Walking with God in the Garden

Journey to *Jouissance*

James McReynolds
Minister of Joy to the World

Parson's Porch Books

Walking with God in the Garden: Journey to Jouissance
ISBN: Softcover 978-1-955581-04-2
Copyright © 2021 by James McReynolds

All rights reserved. No part of this book may be reproduced or transmitted in any form or by any means, electronic or mechanical, including photocopying, recording, or by any information storage and retrieval system, without permission in writing from the publisher.

Parson's Porch Books is an imprint of Parson's Porch & Company (PP&C) in Cleveland, Tennessee. PP&C is an innovative organization which raises money by publishing books of noted authors, representing all genres. Its face and voice is **David Russell Tullock** (dtullock@parsonsporch.com).

Parson's Porch & Company *turns books into bread & milk* by sharing its profits with the poor.

www.parsonsporch.com

Walking with God in the Garden

Contents

Dedication To Dr. David Russell Tullock 7
Foreword by Dr. John Killinger 9
Introduction 11
Chapter One 16
    Tending The Garden Of The Soul
Chapter Two 24
    Biblical Concepts Of Garden
Chapter Three 40
    Prayer In The Garden
Chapter Four 55
    Soil For The Soul
Chapter Five 62
    Sowing the Seed
Chapter Six 72
    Sowing And Reaping
Chapter Seven 81
    Pulling Weeds And Pruning Roses
Chapter Eight 90
    Living With *Jouissance* In The New Garden
Bibliography 103
About the Author 106

Dedication
To Dr. David Russell Tullock

who in retirement continues to proclaim Christ as a publisher. Without his encouragement this author would not be enabled to share the joy of the Lord with the world.

Foreword by Dr. John Killinger

My dear friend James McReynolds knows more about joy than anyone else I have ever known. He became joy's apostle years ago. He has been absorbed with the subject ever since.

In this beautiful book, which is about gardens and beauty, and joy, he leads us at last to a chapter on *jouissance*, a French word for extreme and ultimate joy. It is where he is headed in his life journey all these years.

I know his readers will find themselves transported to this wonderful heart of joy with him, for his very language reflects on every page his adoration of God and what it means to live with the Divine throbbing through every bit of the universe.

I can't even imagine what it would be like to be Jim and to live constantly with this vibrancy at the very center of my entire being.

If anybody was ever prepared to enter heaven, it is Jim. I can't believe that he will find life any richer or more beautiful when he gets there than it was before he left the earth. If anyone ever lived with what one old hymn called "the foretaste of glory," it is he. This book is radiant proof of it!

John Killinger
Warrenton, Virginia

Introduction

If the way to a man's heart is through his stomach, perhaps the palate can light the way to the soul. My brother David wrote a huge volume on the McReynolds family through generations of people who lived in Scotland and then moved to Northern Ireland. His research revealed that many were farmers.

My family always planted huge gardens. My grandparents breezed through the Great Depression, never having to buy food. They lived in the hallows near Elizabethton, Tennessee. My parents grew huge gardens with corn, cucumbers, beans, tomatoes, squash, turnips, watermelons, okra, peas, radishes, strawberries, blackberries, gooseberries, potatoes, onions, cabbage, and more.

At Harmony Baptist Church in Elizabethton, an old church bulletin related that in the garden of his soul we would plant at least nine rows of produce. The first three rows would be squash. We would work to squash gossip, squash ugly criticism and indifference. He would cultivate three rows of turnips: turn up for church, turn up with a smile, turn up to serve others. He would cultivate three rows of lettuce: let us be faithful, let us be unselfish, and let us love one another.

Gardening connects us to life's natural rhythms, the gifts of each season, the wonder of creation, and our natural world. Our family has experienced the joy of gardening. Many of my ancestors came to America because there was famine in Irish homes. Gardens pull us into the present moment. The hard work of gardening creates loss of a sense of time, especially as we dig away, plant, prune, water, and become faithful and patient.

God has increased patience for food growers each and every day, generation after generation. In the garden we live at a gentle pace. Now that I have grown older, I look at the world and appreciate the slow, gradual changes that are the essence of the garden. God will be patient with us when we fail to grow spiritually. The fires of faith will burn strong, not just lukewarm. There might be time to rekindle the flame. We must not put it off until tomorrow.

As we age, our sense of time grows shorter and shorter. The slowness of plant growth becomes a comfort that helps hold back the speed of life. God told us in the beginning exactly where we would find joy with God on earth. God created humans in God's image. God could have given them a place in an ocean, on top of a mountain range, in a castle or a cave. God chose for us the Garden of Eden, a paradise in which Adam and Eve could live with plants of every kind, vegetables and fruit. God guided them in what they were to do. They planted and cultivated the plants. Working with plants brings us closer to divine presence. We shall know the interconnectedness of living things. Come dwell in your Garden of Eden and find your destiny.

Any book about preparing and eating food would not be complete with a word from Julia Child: "Dining with one's friends and beloved family is certainly one of life's primal and most innocent delights, one that is both soul-satisfying and eternal." (Julia Child, *People Who Love to Eat Are Always the Best People*, p. 65.)

I love gardens. Gardening is an effective metaphor for life. Good farming and gardening needs vision. Without a vision, crops fail. We cannot just buy some seeds and expect a creative garden. What kind of garden can you visualize? Just as life needs a vision quest, as do all living things.

As we walk out the back door, what do you see? We need to make gardening a priority. What can we grow? Pumpkins, green beans, potatoes, strawberries, sweet corn, cucumbers, tomatoes, watermelons, flowers, zucchini, and sunflowers. Trim your list to the things you know you can grow. Most of us have limited space. And we know what we can successfully manage. Visioning life on earth starts by creating a list of what you want to do. Plant seeds that bear the fruit that is important to you.

Good soil is vital. Gardeners and farmers spend time, energy, and expense to improve the soil to create a rich, strong, and durable soil. Manure, compost, and nutrients help create an environment conducive to vibrant growth. The soil of your soul must be prepared. Get the education you need. Obtain the skills that will allow you to achieve your goals. Declutter and get organized. Exercise, eating healthy food, getting enough sleep, and walking with God in the pleasant cool of the garden.

Our earthly joy is essentially "being loved." The quest for joy does not require us to go on long journeys. Everywhere we are surrounded by joy stimulators. Continuing to live in the future robs us of joy in the present. The last movie my departed wife Nancy and I saw together was "The Way We Were." Barbra Streisand sang, "If we had it all to do again, would we? Could we?" These questions summarize our lives.

I know Nancy is walking with God in an incredible garden. One of her gifts to the world was her beautiful flowers. She will enjoy the gardens in heaven as much as her daughter and I enjoyed those heavenly flowers at the Shine of the Immaculate Conception in Washington. We enjoyed the hymn that Nancy sang in my churches with passion: "Turn your eyes upon Jesus. Look full in his wonderful face. All the things of earth will grow strangely dim in the light of his glory and grace." Nancy's first and middle name, Nancy Grace, described who she was. She and our daughter Linda kept the last name McReynolds. We spoke of "the three of us" as our love and closeness being like the Trinity.

We three believed in the promise of heaven. When our thoughts turned to heaven, we knew that even death is nothing compared to the vast *jouissance* of life. Linda was with her mom during her time of cancer and finally her going to heaven where she is whole, pain free, and fully healed.

Our souls enjoy the times our unconscious becomes conscious. I was taking a nap one afternoon. Just before I awakened, I saw Nancy walking toward me in the hall in her eternal mansion. She bore a smile on her face. Her skin looked soft and smooth. Her clothing was classic, perfect for her.

After being given such a clear vision, how could anyone doubt the reality of the Next Place? God's dreams for us go far beyond what the world has to offer. God created us wonderfully unique. We yearn for something more, for something lost. Purposely made for a purpose, we exist at this moment to become perfectly ourselves.

Chapter One

Tending the Garden of The Soul

Tending the sacred garden of our souls is the path to joy. Are we tending the garden of our souls? It is time to take a spiritual hoe and work up the ground with scripture, prayer, gatherings of the people, fellowship, giving, and serving.

Standing before an untilled plot of land is quite amazing. A sower's mind is boggled by all the possibilities. Hours of assessing soil, digging, weeding, watering and planting are now required. With your spade you turn over the dirt. Hard packed soil is loosened. The glory of gardening comes with our hands in dirt, our head in the sun, and the soul one with nature. To tend a garden is to nourish the body and the soul.

We are not alone in tending our soul's soil. God invites us into the growth process. God guides and directs us through it. Sometimes we dig up unpleasant obstacles such as underground rocks. We need to feel God's arms around us, forgiving our foolishness, accepting our human impulses, and our freeing the will, loving us in spite of our weaknesses. God's perfection loves us in our imperfection.

As we dig into the soil and our inner garden, we overturn rubble that we never expected. Spiritual maturity is like watching grass grow. The debris and tangles of old roots and the hidden rock may discourage our digging. Do not ignore the yields to just watching grass and plants, tend them. Pretending that our problems do not exist will not cause them to disappear. Pick up the stones. Untangle the useless roots.

In Nebraska this winter the weather reached 50 degrees below zero with the wind chill factor. There is so much joy when spring finally arrives. The winter of 2021 was an especially extended cold in much of the United States. Farmers and gardeners shouted "hurrah," as temperatures warmed, the ground was thawing, and the trees began budding.

We got out our garden gloves, sharpened our hoes. People looked forward to creating the vegetable gardens, the flower gardens, and the rock gardens. Each garden is a different way to use the garden ground. Gardens require good soil as the purpose is producing food for physical nourishment. Flower gardens need a more delicate soil, and flower plants need more tending than other plants. Rock gardens have no need for a particular type of soil. These are planned spaces for decluttering the landscape and offering walking paths and beautiful rest stops.

Tending a garden means different things to different people. For many, it is a way of life. Growing and harvesting not only puts food on the table. This provides income so people can participate in the global economy. In the Midwest there are some huge farms. Even if there is no ownership in abundant farming land, most everyone tends a garden. Gardeners believe in local, organic produce. They find no greater joy than sitting outside among their blooming plants. Tending a garden reflects the approaches humans take to tending their souls and growing in relationship with God. They feel close to God when working hard, getting their hands dirty in service to God and others. In Cass County, Nebraska, members of churches planted and harvested more than 3,000 pounds of potatoes to give to poor and needy people.

When rain poured down, the cutting and planting of potato bubs, weeding and tending the huge potato garden was delayed. Rain falls on everybody at times. Rain creates mud, inconvenience, discomfort, and brings a mess. When emotional rains flood into our soul, we surmise, "Why did this happen to me?" There is a deep yearning in our souls encouraging us to move from slogging through the muddy ground and afterwards standing in the sunshine following the rain. Hope, patience, and optimism give us spiritual stepping-stones to the gleam of sunlight.

When we can move in the mud with a calm mind, the things that used to feel stressful will be blips on the radar. We find it almost impossible to slow down to the speed of life. The world should have listened to Simon and Garfunkel as they sang, "Slow down, you move too fast. You've got to make the moment last."

My friend Harold Bales, a colleague in my studies at Vanderbilt, once told me, "Jim, you do ministry like two sheets in the wind." During my years in the master of divinity degree program and the doctor of divinity studies, I worked in the office of public relations at the Sunday School Board. I composed more writings for Baptist Press, secular newspapers, radio and television as representative of the board at Ridgecrest Baptist Assembly. My soul was challenged and harassed. Walking in the cool of the prayer garden at the summer assembly brought refreshment.

After I received my doctorate at Vanderbilt, I received a call from Eastside Baptist Church in Evansville, Indiana. It was connected to the American Baptist Churches in the United States. I continued to be ambitious beyond any expectation from God, the church, or anyone else. I spread myself thin. Impatience, anger, and frustration rose inside my soul. There appeared to be no benefit from slowing down the pace, relaxing, or taking time off. I received my doctorate and I felt proud to be called "doctor," and I believed that this would bring me success. That was in 1972. In just a bit more than a year, I suffered from exhaustion and clinical depression. I was hospitalized at Deaconess Hospital in Evansville. I reflected on the time in my book *Dancing* with *Bipolar Bears*.

I felt all alone as the door of the psychiatric unit clanged shut. The first thing I remember was a nurse who brought me the best chicken I ever tasted. She said, "Nobody can hurt you here." I was released in 1973. My wife Nancy and daughter Linda moved to Sant Joseph, Missouri. Immediately I started working in mental health at the Saint Joseph State Hospital. And then against my wife's wishes, I accepted a call, and served ten years as pastor for Pilgrim Presbyterian Church in Cameron, Missouri.

My pace did not slow down. I foolishly said, "I'd rather burn out than rust out." It was a way of life for me. I continued to struggle with this frustrating way of life.

I kept running with exhaustion, weakness, and pain in moving through each day. These unhealthy results have had little effect with my overactive, fluttering butterfly mind that thinks too much, worries too much, and produces brain fog. Sensitive people take in more than any person could possibly do.

A woman in Weeping Water gave me a nice plague with the red Disciples cup and white cross. On it she wrote, "Being a Disciple is not a matter of credentials or success, but it is following Jesus with a willing heart." In my more than ten years as pastor of the First Christian Church in Weeping Water, we had 12 small groups going. Our congregation enjoyed 101 baptisms in ten years. I received another plague for my service as moderator of the Nebraska regional board of the Christian Church.

Words similar to these were prayed over me at the Saint Benedict Conference Center where Disciples of Christ hold a retreat every January. "We will never find our worth in achievements, having a world-shaking presence. Our souls are already loved more than enough in God."

We have a need to focus on our small furrow in the garden as we walk with God. Slow and steady is the wise way to the finishing line. God does not want us to check with those beside us or behind us, or in front of us who are on their own journeys.

God asks us to come aside and rest a while. Your inner soul does not stop functioning. Every contribution adds to our joy. What matters most is our walk with God. Staying faithful may mean pausing sometimes. Our soul's attitude means everything as God supplies the strength, the joy, the energy, wisdom, and faith that we need.

The psalmist told us to surrender our soul to God. "Surrender your anxiety. Be silent and stop your striving and you will see that I am God. I am the God above the nations, and I will be exalted throughout the whole earth." Psalm 46:10.

Ministers act like the hare in Aesop's story. We are not as receptive as we want to be to God's pleas for slowing down to repair, discern, and rest. We are encouraged by spiritual strivers to act more like the tortoise.

As we grow older, the truth of getting lost is vivid. The other day I took my 2010 Toyota for service. The back fender had fallen off in the winter snow. I took it to Lincoln by way of 84th Street and Yankee Hill Road. When I went to leave, I got lost in Lincoln. There was a detour up 84th and I drove nearly one hundred miles to find my way out of Lincoln. In my ministry while living in Elmwood, I have share joy in every county and in churches of all kinds in Nebraska. I know it is important not to hurry. I have anecdotal evidence, but I have observed that hurrying leads to trouble.

Once we stop rushing, it is amazing how much joy we become aware of missing. Gardening simply does not allow a person to become mentally old. Too many hopes and dreams are yet to be realized. We grow flowers and plants for different reasons. Gardens are pleasing to the eye. Tending a garden pleases the soul. For some it may be for the novelty or the nostalgia. Most of us just enjoy seeing them grow.

Whatever your age, slow down. You'll see the beauty of the earth and enjoy the moment. Without self-awareness, we cannot change. God has spoken to me all during my life. In 1975 I vowed to preach at least one sermon every single day. God shakes the Divine head in laughter after almost 50 years of this unnecessary use of my time.

The feeling of being rushed has saturated my work. Do you measure success by your levels of achievements? We want to stay on top. We have created more time stress. Our physical health is damaged. Being intimate with God, our family, our community, and our church will yield loving environments.

Slowing down is worth the serenity and peace of mind. Peace is not a reward for winning a race. Walking with God means to become aware of your thinking. It is so frustrating to not know what to do. As I scrambled to find my way out of Lincoln, I stopped and asked for directions, but I continued to be lost. I found that I made a left turn at one point instead of a right turn. Slowing down makes us sharper. Life is as unpredictable as is the solution. Lost souls are trapped in the past. They can't realize that the present is all we have.

Stress and finally exhaustion originates in our thinking. Being present in relationships with God and other living beings brings intimacy. We cannot have loving relationships if we keep traveling at the speed of light. Have we lost hope deep in our souls that relationships can be magically healed? Those who discover *jouissance* do one thing at a time, see their moods with compassion, accept each moment, live in trust, and work smarter not harder. Slow down the pace like basketball teams do when they sense a possible runaway or upset because the team cannot control the pace.

During the Reformation, Martin Luther said, "I have held many things in my hands, and I have lost them all. Whatever I have placed in God's hands, that I still possess."

Chapter Two

Biblical Concepts of Garden

As it was in the time of Adam and Eve, the garden remains a paradise created by God for God's beloved creatures. There is little reference to the Genesis story in the remainder of the Hebrew scriptures. The garden in Eden was a place of flourishing fertility. Cultivation of the land and gardening are woven into the story in Genesis. God planted a garden for humans to live in and enjoy. The best way to find God is in the garden. At the end of the day, no matter what our age, we are all looking for a deeper sense of purpose and connection with God and creation.

Every day is the beginning or the first something. In children, we celebrate progress. We hug them, applaud them, kiss them, and reward them for the tiniest of advances. Encouragement plays a huge role in their lives. Who we ae today is just a shadow of who we are capable of with God. Our potential excites and frustrates us.

The biblical concept of the creation of humanity points to love. The man Adam (the word for human being) was made from the dust of the ground. The breath of life animated him. Life comes with breath and stops when breath departs. The plot of the story hinges on the idea that God does not want humanity to eat from the tree of knowledge. Adam is not initially forbidden to eat from the tree of life. Unhappiness is the fruit of choosing, saying, and doing that which contradicts who we were destined to be.

The old proverbial plot thickens when God decrees that "it is not good that the male should be alone." Adam is allowed to name all the animals, but no animal was a fit partner. In the end, Adam finds a partner in the woman who is formed from his rib. Paul argues in I Corinthians 11:8-9 that man was created first. A more careful reading of Genesis reveals a bond between man and woman In Genesis 2.

In the Near East even today, the assumption is that females should defer to males.

The man and the woman were naked but never ashamed. This thought brings us to the sexual overtones. Some congregations teach that the "knowledge of good and evil" refers to sexuality. In Genesis 4:1, the story says that after their expulsion from Eden, Adam knew his wife, Eve, and she conceived and bore Cain. "To know" means to have sexual relations.

Genesis 3 introduces the serpent as craftier than any other created animal. The book of Revelation refers to the ancient serpent as Satan, the deceiver of the world. The serpent leads the human couple to question God's prohibition against eating from the tree of knowledge of good and evil. The woman eats the forbidden fruit. She offers it to Adam. The consequences were quite severe. We call it the Fall. Genesis 3:14-19 focuses on the words to the serpent, the woman, and the man.

These were the assumptions about the nature of life. The story is a view of the female condition. There is no hope of any meaningful life after death. Before Christ, the Hebrew Bible indicated that after death all people, good and bad, went to a shadowy underworld called Sheol. The Greek counterpart was called Hades.

Theological Misconceptions

The chapter in Genesis has been interpreted with bias in the church. Augustine brought the concept of original sin. This belief shared with many is that human beings after Adam were born in a state of sin. The Genesis story is paradigmatic, as the story of the temptation to eat forbidden fruit is typical of all human experience. As is the inclination to sin inherited from one generation, the Bible makes no suggestion here that guilt is transmitted genetically.

Equally misinterpreted is that the responsibility for sin lay with Eve rather than with Adam. Was Eve approached first because she was weaker? Adam bears the primary responsibility. The decree about the fruit of the garden in Eden was made before Eve was created. Adam and Eve suffered equally from the consequence of their acts.

The story in Genesis is compelling. The lure of forbidden fruit is of high interest.
Adam has free range over most of the garden. The limit imposed by God is crucial. Obedience to a higher authority is essential in the biblical account.

The plot of Genesis is that humans relate to God. They relate to themselves. The relate to others. There is no escape the ripple effects of the decisions of others whether you choose them or not. We relate to the earth where we live. We gather food from earth. Our habits and decisions have consequences for the environment. The plot of the story ends in Genesis 2: "Adam and his wife were naked and felt so shame." Shame was never in their conscious. In their Fall, they felt like a heavy velvet curtain at the end of a play. God appeared distant, lacking trust, and unknowable. The negative emotions humans attempt to escape were introduced. Effortless love became effortless competition. Their offspring resorted to violence as self-protection, self-exaltation, and self-indulgence emerged. No longer was the earth in perfect cooperation. Earth was cursed with airborne disease and hard soil that required harder work.

The Garden of Eden is portrayed as a historical place. By word and deed, God demonstrated love in Eden. The story begins in peace and bounty. It then speaks about divine judgment. Humans were given dominion above all other created beings.

Human work and their calling were joyful. It was not a burden. The garden was beautiful. In this perfect setting, they fractured their fellowship by doing the one thing God told them not to do. The biblical account of Eden shows the depth of the kindness of God. With everything they needed, Adam and Eve selfishly grasped for more. They were held responsible for exchanging a dream for a nightmare.

Without this story giving a glimpse of what Eden was, humans cannot fully understand the Lord's rich provision with our repentance and faith. Christ Jesus was sent to earth to reverse the alienation caused by what we call the fall. The saga begins when God inserted the divine into the story to recover the plot. Jesus demonstrated how we are to live. Only God could heal the walls that elevate human agendas above anyone else including God. Jesus came to save us from the separateness that keeps us from the kingdom, the New Eden prepared for us as the redeemed.

In John's Revelation, his writing inspired by God, places a river and fruit-bearing trees in the middle of God's New Eden, the Holy City. Revelation 22:2. This is the destiny of those redeemed in Jesus where human beings will again experience abundance, safety, intimacy, and assurance from God.

Eating from the tree of knowledge of good and evil in Genesis conceptualized the duality of good and evil in our own consciences. We understand that we create evil by giving our energy to it in thought, word, and deed. A shift of giving our energy to love and to bless, prosper, and heal will usher in a new Garden of Eden as we return to God. We can return to the garden and walk with God in the cool of the day, intimacy without words.

The garden as metaphor for life

The biblical concept of garden is about beginnings and flourishing. The Word of God teaches about the rhythms of living on the earth. The garden reminds us of a decaying world. The garden is a place where we find shade, cool air in times of heat, comfort when we become sad or depressed. It is rest from our work. As a soil and life giver, the earth sustains us. A flower garden is a source of joy. Bonding with the earth provides profound insights. Every day on our life journey we live in a garden, and we are gardeners with God.

In the beginning, we survey the land, till the soil, dig into the land, and shape our part of the earth as a Garden of Eden. The garden is a place for beginnings, for pruning, removing weeds, and seeding. Sometimes our garden is comfortable but not pretty, a dwelling place for growing old. Is growing old a product of eating the wrong food? Adam and Eve came to realize that they were aging. At each year we are given, we will bear spiritual fruit. The seasons pass and blend with one another. We can continue to bear a riper, fuller fruit, not at all possible when we were young twigs. We give wisdom, secrets, and insights culled from living even beyond the biblical three score and ten years. The gardening years teach us the mutuality between the Creator and humankind.

The Bible is filled with garden metaphors. The word "faith" is used nearly 300 times in scripture. To eat is used 800 times. Except for Mary finding Jesus at his tomb, most of the time Jesus appeared at meals such as in the Upper Room, on the Emmaus Road, or the fish fry on the edge of the Sea of Galilee.

During seminary most students, at least in past years, studied Hebrew. Hebrew is a concrete language. The Hebrew Bible offers helpful solutions in the form of symbols and stories when discussing things that matter. Paradoxical language puts two contradictory words together to express an idea that neither word could express on its own. Good grief or painful joy are examples.

Jesus knew the scripture quite well. His preaching was plain and concrete. Jesus taught tax collectors, Samaritans, divorced women, prostitutes, and estranged people. His parables centered on food and eating. His stories were for insight and vision. Those who heard him had to make serious decisions about what the stories Jesus told could mean.

Jesus was not the first person that blessed bread and wine during a meal. This was part of the Essene community of his time and the Jewish customs. Feasting was his image for the kingdom of God.

The Hebrew scripture tells us that when God created the world, the tree was a symbol of life and death, of good and evil. Human limits are symbolized in a tree. God does not reveal which tree is the tree of life. Theologians have attempted to figure this out. Nobody has come up with an answer.

The apple tree is what we often associate with this garden of Eden tree. Others conclude grapes, citron, or a fig tree. Adam and Eve covered themselves with fig leaves when they discover that are naked in the aftermath of disobeying God. The tree was chosen as the life-form as an example for humans. The first thing God does in the garden is to plant trees. Does it matter what kind of tree? God wants us to follow by planting trees. The more trees we plant, the more we learn about how to enjoy them and how to care for them. The Bible's concepts of garden and God's intentions are summarized in Deuteronomy 33:18 as a blessing from Moses to the 12 tribes: "And Israel shall dwell securely alone, Jacob's blessing, in a land of grain and wine, and the heavens will drip dew." Readers, we have shared our historical journey with culinary expressions. Moses gave a strange blessing. What blessing is there "to dwell securely alone?" What does he mean by "the heavens will drip dew?"

Some theologians explain that each individual will live under his own vine and fig tree. The people will be transformed in order that they will not live clustered together in groups or in cities and towns. Humans will feel safe to spread themselves throughout the land. Isaac's blessing of "dew of the heavens" was added to Jacob's blessing.

Using the words, "land of grain and wine," is a harbinger to human reinstating the earth into a new Garden of Eden. God's people are to impart this blessing onto the land. God will give us the power to restore the garden during our earthly journey.

The biblical stories answer the question, "Who am I" The saga moves beyond accepting ourselves and loving God like God loves us. What is the fruit of this knowledge? In Genesis 12:2, God tells Abraham, "I will bless you." Despite everything that is negative in the stories, some have pointed to original innocence rather than original sin as an explanation. Love is the essence of who we are and who God is. Blessings of Abram and every person are like a rock thrown across a creek causes rippling of the water. The stone sinks. The energized rock radiates on to the shore. As God has filled us with blessings in our living soul, we become more in tune with God and ourselves.

The words soul and spirit are used in differing biblical contexts. The word nephesh is found more than 780 times in the Hebrew scriptures. In the Greek New Testament psyche is used 103 times.

Soul is used as describing an individual person. Ezekiel declared that the soul that sins will die. Ezekiel 18:20. Peter wrote centuries later that eight souls were saved by water in the days of Noah. I Peter 3:20. Genesis indicates that soul is life itself. Genesis 1:30. The Genesis story references life as biological life. That life is common in animals and humans. All creatures have life.

In the book of Revelation, creatures living in the sea were said to have a soul. Revelation 8:9. In the biblical record, a soul could refer to the mind. It is the emotional and intellectual part of humankind. Genesis 27:15. The concept of humans being made in the image of God, indicates souls exist apart from the physical body. Matthew 10:28, Revelation 6:9.

What is the biblical concept of the human spirit? The Hebrew word ruach (breath or wind) is used 378 times. The Greek word pneuma occurs just one more time, 379 times. The word is the basis for the English word pneumonia. Spirit takes on different senses depending on the context. Spirit can denote a person's breath. It also means wind.

Spirit is used as a non-physical being. God the Father is called a spirit. John 4:24. The Trinity includes the Holy Spirit. The biblical view may be interpreted as spirit equals soul. Paul used the "inner person" in II Corinthians 4:16. Spirit is a synonym of soul.

Spirit is used to describe a mental state. It is an attitude for good or evil. Read I Timothy 1:7, I Peter 3:4, and Galatians 6:1. A research of these terms shows that no one has or holds to any one definition of soul or spirit. Biblical words must be examined in their context.

Does God Have a Soul?

The entire biblical writings expressed the concept of soul. Adam and Eve were created uniquely when comparing humankind to the rest of creation. God created humanity as "living souls." Soul is mentioned in the Psalms. Read Psalm 62:5 and 104:1. Luke 1:46 has Mary saying, "My soul magnifies the Lord." The Bible reveals that we are made in God's image. Does that mean that God has a soul?

Two biblical accounts that indicate that God has a soul are Leviticus 26:11 and Judges 10:16. In both the Hebrew word nephesh is used in connection to God. In Jeremiah 34:41, God makes a promise concerning Israel. "I will in doing them good and will plant them in this land with my heart and soul." God is thought to have a hand and a face. And hind parts! Explanations of theologians is that explanations about God's soul are anthropomorphisms. Writers are attributing the characteristics of God like bodily features. John 4:24 reveals, "God is spirit and those who worship God worship in spirit and truth." We find no scripture that says that God is a soul or that God possesses a soul. Soul is difficult to define. Perhaps rather than saying we have a soul, perhaps it is clearer to say that we are a soul.

God does express feelings and emotions. We may say God is not without soul. People of every religion have difficulty understanding what we call the trinity. In Genesis 1:26-29, God said, "Let us make humankind in our image, in our likeness, so that they may rule over the fish in the sea and the birds in the sky, over the livestock and all the wild animals, and over all the creatures that move along the ground." John 1:1 reminds us that the Father is God from the beginning. In John 10:30, Jesus reveals himself as equal to the Father. Together, they sent us the Holy Spirit. Read I John 5:7-11. Logically and mysteriously, God does not have a soul. God is a soul, a single soul in three persons.

When Jesus became human, he was body and soul. His journey to live on earth, Jesus lived a human experience. Jesus took on human form, so he had a body and a soul. Humans can interpret this to mean soul is about the essence and being of God.

"In the beginning," or "once upon a time." The phase offers mystery and promise. It's our nature to long to know ancient things. We enjoy finding our roots. Eternity has been placed in our souls. There is the "beginning" used here and again in John. We could interpret the words to say, "Once upon eternity."

Some African American spiritual songs cited God as lonely. We image God sitting on a throne. We do wonder like children, "How did all the things in the world get here? Why is there people, animals, and plants, and flowers? When?
Where? Who?" In God's image, we desire to belong, to be a part of life, and to be invited to participate. Humans naturally desire to be a part of a family, or in fellowship with friends.

All life preceded us. What a gift to have our own ancestral roots reveal who we are. The story reveals that life has always been good. To our surprise, we find that our stories are something grand. In John 17:24, we are assured that we were loved from the beginning of all creation. We need to know if love lasts. Death or divorce or dejection ends a story. The past is lost and can never be recovered. The future is full of anxiety and uncertainty. Photos are stripped from photo books. Pictures come off the walls. The self-centered life brings disappointment. There was a life before we existed.

Imagine the most beautiful scene ever seen. Imagine the beginning of the Rocky Mountains, the Alps, rain forests, flowers in bloom, and all living things in the beginning. Job 38:7 reveals that "the morning stars sang together, and all the angels shouted for joy." God is more creative than we can imagine. Women and men were created with such lovely bodies that a kiss tastes delicious. Only lovers fully know this marvel. Think of the best kiss you ever experienced. The body was created so we are able to enjoy sex. Review that life video lifting the love scene out of time and place, and you will be viewing Eden. Women long to be beautiful. Men want to be brave. All humans want this reality. "Made in the image of God" means we have imagination, the ability to reason and choose, to create, to share intimacy, and to know joy.

Satan was the source of the reason we reached out to the fruit. Our eternal souls were deceived, and humans fell from grace. By the sixth chapter of the Genesis story, human evil reached the point where God could bear it any longer. Genesis 6:5-6.

Humans have failed in the most essential thing which is love. Something is wrong with the world, with us, with life. Eden has been lost. Satan and even our fellow human beings seduce us, deceive us, and misrepresent themselves, with whatever seduces us into darkness. A woman softly says, "The better to seduce you with my dear." The human race is captive in the worst way possible.

God cannot save us as we have no idea how captive we are. We cannot know how desperate people have become. Our souls long for a new Eden. We hesitate to surrender to God. God took on human flesh in the coming of Jesus. We came without his inherited glory, in humility, and he whispers his words to all lovers, "I have come to you not to seduce you, but to unconditionally love you." God in Jesus gave his life. A Roman soldier says at the cross, "Surely this man was a son of God." The soldier understands the story now. God's love is fully revealed by the life, death, and resurrection of Jesus.

As Jesus laid down his life for us, he was laid inside a tomb. His burial was like any other dead person. His family and friends mourned. Mark 16:2-7 reveals a dramatic turn. Jesus came back to the living earth. In his resurrected body, he asked to eat. His resurrection is the forerunner of our own restoration. We shall exist in a new Eden. In our restoration, we will walk in the garden in the cool of the day together with God. We will see Jesus face to face. Our childhood questions will be answered. God does not want even one of us to perish. God is loving and patient. God does not want to lose us. God still wants us to live in a new Eden. Salvation is the restoration of life as it was always meant to be. The new Eden will be immortal. Paradise will not be lost again. Nothing can take it away. On the Nebraska plains, the sunrise and the sunset help us to remember Eden's glory that promises Eden's return.

Our long years of exile will be swept away in the joy-filled tears of our arrival home.

The Garden of Eden is restored.

God has established eternity in our souls. Our own story puts grace and love into words and images. The story is filled with suffering and longing. It is a story of hope. Our eyes well up in tears and get a glimpse of unspeakable joy.

The "joy of the Lord" gives us a taste of Eden in this life journey. We may be one of the fortunate ones who find a bit of love and happiness. We lose our health. Age conquers us. Family, friends, and loved ones slip from our hands. Our work, our calling will remain unfinished. Everyone on earth today will breathe a last breath.

The Good News is that God placed eternity in our souls. Eternity is written in our hearts. Revelation 21:1 declares that there will be a new heaven and a new earth." In the twinkling of an eye, humankind will be restored. Lovers and those beloved by us will be reunited. Paradise is regained.

Some hearty Nebraskans really enjoy winter. Winter does have its joys. We wonder at the beauty of snow, the rush of a sled going down a hill, the magic of the winter holidays, the fireplace, the time and activity done indoors. Nebraska is said to have two seasons: shovel and sweat. If climate changed and winter never left, how sad it would be for us. The trees would not grow back their leaves. The grass would remain dry and brittle. Cold, silent, and bleak would describe the earth forever.

Most of us long for the return of spring and summer. It is the season of sweating. Gardens will blossom. Fields yield corn and beans. The meadows appear soft and green. The restoration of Eden is played out before us each spring and summer. God is giving Eden back to us.

"All the days ordained for me were written in your book before one of them came to be." Psalm 139:16. We often say as we get older, "Where did the time go?" Once the time of our earthly journey is gone, it is gone. Our days are numbered. We hold the propensity to spend and waste time on things that just do not matter. These are the things of eternal value.

Each of us has a God-given ability to architect our lives. None of us knows exactly how many days we have left. Imagine that thoughts rode down the path of being judgmental, negative, critical, complaining, and worrisome. Stop and choose something true, honest, just, pure, lovely and of good report. Philippians 4:8.

Chapter Three

Prayer in The Garden

A garden needs attention, love, and careful pruning. The practice of prayer requires the same. When we pray and garden, we build a relationship with God. As we strengthen our prayer, our words and thoughts rise from the fertile soil of our souls.

I have a new appreciation for the hymn "In the Garden" composed in 1913 by Charles Austin Miles. (*Chalice Hymnal*, hymn number 227)

"I come to the garden alone, While the dew is still on the roses, And the voice I hear falling on my ear, The Son of God discloses."

The refrain: "And He walks with me, and He talks with me, And He tells me I am His own; And the joy we share as we tarry there, none other has even known."

The next two verses read: "He speaks, and the sound of His voice is so sweet the birds hush their singing, and the melody that He have to me within my heart is ringing. I'd stay in the garden with Him, though the night around me is falling, but He bids me go; through the voice of woe His voice to me is calling."

A Nebraska farmer has this prayer in his barn. It was often used by monks in the 12th century: "Oh Lord Jesus, true gardener, work in us what you want of us, for you are the true gardener, at once maker and tiller, and keeper of your garden. God, you who plant with the Word, water with the Spirit, and give your increase with your power."

Pray for protection. Pray verbally. Pray scripture over the mind. God will help you transform negative thoughts and renew your mind. Romans 12:2. Paul encourages us to keep a heavenly perspective. Philippians 4:6-7. Pray that we never have to wage a war with a deadly virus. Many people crumble under soul splintering conditions. Turnaround from panic reactions, and pivot over the panic. Rehearse the goodness of God daily. Piano players know practice makes perfect or permanent. Rehearsing fears and negative outcomes lead to panic.

Reframe worry into prayer. Anxiety and prayer are opposites. Anxiety and worry face off against gratitude and trust. Reframe those fearful thoughts into prayers. Pray it out in the presence of God. When we come into agreement with God, heaven responds. We receive the promise of peace when we let go and let God. Prayer reassures us in times of trouble. God's peace settles our weary souls with the renewing of our minds.

Prayer unites us in our shared humanity. Prayer is a gift from God to help us communicate with the divine. Prayer comes without a specific time, place or method. Confession, thanksgiving, intercession, worship, and praise as heaven touches earth with grace. Frances DeSales noted, "Prayer is the most effective means for cleansing the mind and emotions. This is because it places the mind in God's bright light and the emotions in his warm love. Prayer is like water that makes plants grow and extinguishes fires."

Those fires may be something that happened in the past. If they were hurt in relationships, they cannot live in love and joy today. Once we perform something we are sorry for, we are certain that we are bad. Anger from the past causes us to hold on to self-righteousness. We do not want to forgive and forget. Because we may have stolen something, so we punish ourselves forever. We just cannot resist playing the videos of our past. Today is the only moment we can experience. Walking with God in prayer can enable us to clean up the past. Prayer can release us from our emotional attachments. As we let go of those limiting memories, we are free to use our thinking power to enjoy this moment and to create a better future.

Love is always the answer to healing our souls. The pathway to love is forgiving and letting go. Forgiveness resolves resentment. Put away the old thoughts. We can never change them. Feel the easing joy of letting go. The only think we can control is our current thoughts. Old thinking will attempt to come back. We can say, "I now choose to believe it is becoming easier to make changes." Listen to the conversation with your mind several times for the mind to acknowledge that we are in control. Live never happens as we imagine it. Thoreau told us that our life journeys are filled with "quiet desperation." Young people do not think, "I do hope my life will be one of quiet desperation. Perhaps somebody will help me make a plan that will lead me into the desperate kind of life."

Each moment brings a new beginning. We are never stuck. Transformation of our soul happens here and now. We begin to make a shift today. God has given us authority and power in the earth where we live. Beliefs and thoughts from the past created this moment. Ask God to support us in new choices to bring joy in the next moment and the next day, the next month, or the next year. Thoughts move swiftly. In walking with God in prayer, we can watch and listen to what we are saying. As negative thoughts of any sort invade us, stop them. There is no time to waste.

God sent us to earth to transcend our limitations. We are here for recognizing our magnificence no matter what people tell us. Our visit to this world is like going to school. Tests and grades in school only show how much knowledge we had at a given time. They do not measure our worth. Love is everywhere. We are made to be lovable and loving. Loving people who are with us on our journey will become more loving towards us. God has designed a world where what we give out, we get back.

We create our own situations. We give our power away as we blame others for our frustration. No person, place, or thing has power over us. We are the only thinkers in that scene. When we create peace and harmony and balance in our minds, we will discover it in our lives.

During prayer time, we quiet our soul and allow "the joy of the Lord" to surface. We can ask God, "What do I need to know?" Wait quietly for an answer. Prayer connects us to God where we find unlimited possibilities to explore. If one avenue does not work, try another. We use our earthly possessions for a brief life journey. At our death, they pass on to somebody else. Our books, our sermons, our records of our family, our homes, our cars, everything goes. There is a natural flow to our lives. People and things go and come. When something goes, it is making room for something more.

Rejoice each morning in the abundance of awakening for another new day. As we walk through the dew and the morning glories and the roses, we experience the joy of being alive, being healthy, having friends, being able to create, and to become an example of what the kingdom of joy brings.

What do we hope to achieve by prayer? Wisdom, comfort, energy, place, healing come with prayer. The more willing we are to sit in quiet contemplation, the more prepared we are to listen to the still, soft voice within us. Approach prayer time as having an intimate conversation with a friend. Like planting seeds in the soil, prayer will enable us to establish a habit of praying that goes deeper and deeper each time we pray. Farmers in the Midwest speak of the joy of sitting back and hearing the crops grow. Any minute there is growing below the soil, nestled in our souls. Prayer is about words. Prayer is watching and listening for the responses that come to us, so subtly that we will miss them if we are not paying attention.

Later, I shall write about things that damage the most cherished garden. Nebraska experienced a huge flood in 2019 that destroyed everything in its wake. We are vigilant of hungry animals, weeds, floods, and things that tear us away from our inner living souls. Prayer brings wisdom from something other than the world outside the soul. Always be ready to lift up prayers. The seeds of wisdom, acceptance, healing, comfort, and energy are qualities to sustain us and encourage us.

Blessing Gardens and Gardeners

Churches in rural Nebraska take time to bless the soil, the seeds, water, and farming tools. They prayer for seeds: "Creating God, you have given seed for the sower. Protect, nourish, and bless the bulbs and seeds which are sown in hope. May these life seeds bring bountiful fruit and beauty. Amen."

Great faith is needed to plant a tree that only the next generation will see. She who plants a garden plants hope. To plant a tree is to believe in the future.

Nebraska farmland has been called a Garden of Eden. On the very top of the state capitol in Lincoln is a sower sowing seeds. The Nebraska state legislature begins with prayers including appreciation for the soil, water and rain. While serving churches in Pawnee City, Tecumseh, Weeping Water, and Nebraska City, I have enjoyed writing out prayers blessing gardens and gardeners, expressing gratitude for the soil, water, and growth in the Cornhusker state legislature.

Each prayer is recorded in the minutes of the legislature. One example: "God, you planted your garden called Eden, come and bless the soil which is our garden. All that dies becomes earth, and it lives again. Make us realize that one day your garden will be our final bed of love and joy. Amen."

Let us thank God for gardens: "Graceful Lord, in creation, you made earth a garden. You entrusted us to till and to keep a place of peace and beauty where we can walk with you. Through redemption, the One who died for us was buried in a garden. There you raised him up to give us hope and risen life. Through the Church, you tend us as a garden, a place of abundant harvest, where we are work with you. Meet us, we pray, in all the gardens where we go for refreshment and prayer. Bless the garden of your Church. Guide those who plant and tend it. Make us fruitful in ministry and mission. Bless all the gardens of our community, the shelter of families, the fragrance of friendship. In our care for one another, cause us to grow in love and wisdom, in gentleness, in kindness, in joy. Amen."

Prayer is communion with God. Communing is "to converse together, usually intensely and intimately, interchanging feelings and thoughts." People are geared to pray when they are in trouble or they want something. We call out to friends only when we want something or need help. God desires a love relationship with us. Whining or praising are the major themes as humans pray. Prayer is best when we have a grateful heart, knowing that what we ask for is already ours. The Word of God speaks of God's ear being attentive to the righteous. Surely all prayers are heard. The answers may not be recognized or accepted, but each answer is best for we who pray. Jesus went to a garden early in the morning to pray. He realized that the Father was the ultimate source of all life.

The goodness of food is a source of joy. We are in relationship with the entire earth community. We can never escape our link to earth. Humans are interdependent with the animals, the plants, and the living land. While we live on earth, we cannot shed our bodies. There is joy in relating to God and others through eating, making love, conversations, and exercising together. Glory comes in our relationship with the community of earth. We enjoy all the delights it provides. Wisdom arrives as we grow some of our own food. We can eat organic food. We can buy food locally.

Even those alienated from formal religion will bow their heads and pause for prayer. One family or individual says grace, and another gives thanks, and others a table blessing. The structure of these blessings is glorifying and acknowledging the goodness and might of God. The gift of food comes as we smell delight and as we wait to sit down and eat. Saying grace is an impulse to trust, to surrender control, and to know joy. Grace reminds children that they are loved and nourished, assured of the goodness of God. Saying grace teaches children to join hands in a community that expresses delight in one another in the family, and to respond to the gracious gifts from God spontaneously and simply with unrestrained delight. Children will never forget the saying of grace. Generations of grace saying will follow for thousands of years. Often families say a simple grace like: "God is great. God is good. Let us thank God for our food." During summer church camp, we may say: "Oh the Lord has been good to us, and so we thank the Lord for giving us the things we need, the sun and the rain and the apple seed, for every seed we grow, another tree will grow, and soon there will be an orchard there for everyone in the world to share. Amen."

Before we built a new home, there was an apple tree among the forest of trees on our lot of land. Tasting the apples or making an apple pie was a miracle. We gave away many delicious apples and shared apples for the community food bank for others to enjoy.

Enjoy walking with God in God's presence. Notice what you see, what you feel, what you sense. Feel your feet in each step. Walking is a prayer that triggers thoughts. See in every direction the blue in the sky, the vibrant color in the flowers that grow freely, the insects squirming along your path. Drink in the taste of the air. The life-giving miracles of our senses are gifts from God. As we stroll for our soul, we sharpen our awareness, as we focus on one sense at the time. Walk tall, lift your head, notice the motion of your body, and allow the spirit to lift with your body. Hear the crackle of leaves beneath your walking feet. Smell the wet grass and the dew, the trees, and the soil. When we heighten our senses, we heighten awareness.

Thank God for your body's ability to touch, smell, see, hear, and taste. As you walk you will sharpen your senses and wonder in the gifts of sensual awareness. Pray with imagination. When shooting free throws, I imagine the ball tossed high and soft into the basket. I cannot explain it, but magical power comes as we imagine anything as completed, already given.

When words escape us, flowers speak. One of the most joyful times with my daughter Linda was on a day-long tour of the Basilica of the National Shrine of the Immaculate Conception in Washington. It is the largest church in the United States. It is the tallest habitable building in Washington. We marveled looking at the Byzantine Revival and Romanesque architecture.

The basilica contains 81 prayer chapels. The interior contains domes in Grecian styles and decorated in mosaics. Built in the style of medieval churches, the shine relies on masonry walls and columns in place of steel and concrete. More than 10,000 worshipers could walk with God there. Linda and I enjoyed a meal in the basement cafeteria. There are hidden public address speakers to carry the sound of a sermon or speech at the altar pulpit throughout the building.

The prayer gardens contain thousands of flowers. The religious monks who serve there are Franciscans. Saint Francis spoke to the flowers, the trees, and the moon and sun. The flowers spoke to Francis' soul. There were many colors and varieties of roses that symbolized God at work. The intricate and elegant rose offers a glimpse of God's presence in creation. As the fragrant flower blooms, its buds slowly open to reveal the lovely layers. One of the monks told us how spiritual wisdom is illustrated in the blooming rose. The sweetness of love comes to mind in the smell of the rose, reminding us of the love of God. Our tour guide revealed that miracles and encounters with angels have involved roses.

The rose reminds us of our messed-up lives. They represent how complicated we are. Its velvety texture and colors are accompanied by prickly thorns that can draw blood. The path to ultimate joy is a horny path. In the prayer garden we deal with the parts of ourselves that cause pain as well as the parts that spread joy.

Complex polarities exist together like the petals of the rose. We are connected as means of grace to bring the love of God. Roses radiate love. In walking with God, we are invited to participate in the miraculous nurturing of the world with God and the angels.

Roses and angels

When communicating with God or an angel people report smelling the fragrance of a rose. Angels use the rose scents as physical signs of their presence. Angelic energy vibrates best in roses. Roses are symbols of miraculous work. Some view the rose as a symbol of the soul. Smelling the fragrance of roses reminds us of spirituality. Roses are a reminder of the Garden of

Eden. The soul is sacred. The rose brings an odor of sanctity. The roses in the prayer gardens white, red, pink, and purple symbolizing differing spiritual concepts.

Morning glories

Morning glories of many colors are found in the shine prayer gardens. Depending on the color of the flower, morning glories hold a deep symbolism of unrequited love. They also represent the mortality of life. There is a legend that indicates that lovers can only meet on one day of the year. The sparkling morning glory opens fragile arms to receive the day. "Weeping may linger for the night, but joy comes with the morning." Psalm 30:5. Without hope we are engulfed in darkness and discouragement. A new day promises miraculous possibilities with the hopeful brilliance of the morning glory.

A white morning glory represents innocence and purity. A red one symbolizes passion. Pink morning glories symbolize romance, gentle feelings, and thoughtfulness toward one who is beloved. Blue morning glories are symbols of respect, trust, and deep soul felt emotions. Purple morning glories symbolize beauty, royalty, and nobility. Praying with morning glories in the garden signifies love that has never ended. Every single morning glory represents a life.

Tulips bring happiness.

People in the Netherlands grow tulips. In Holland and in the holy shine, tulips are signs of eternal love. The shine workers believe that purple tulips mean royalty.

Pink tulips represent happiness. Yellow tulips symbolize cheerful thoughts. White tulips represent forgiveness. Tulips are extremely popular in the Netherlands. National Tulip Day is celebrated in January. One that day tulip growers build a gigantic tulip garden. Visitors are encouraged to pick up a free bouquet of tulips.

Tulips are the flowers for an eleven-year wedding anniversary. There are more than 3,000 varieties of tulips. Red tulips are a favorite among passionate lovers. Their deep hues evoke feelings of *jouissance*, of love and lust, making them quite popular with young adults. The Dutch say red tulips mean "believe me," or "my feelings are honest." When one seeks to seduce somebody, he or she might send an alluring bouquet of red tulips. Orange tulips convey understanding and appreciation during a relationship. Orange tulips give the thought that lovers feel spiritually and physically connected. Yellow tulips represent hope, cheerfulness, and hope. Planting yellow tulips in the garden brings prosperity and good luck. Purple tulips are a symbol of elegance and royalty. Purple tulips are brought into the church during funerals. Purple tulips say, "I am sorry." They are given to each other by the Catholic priests for honoring a spiritual milestone. When we dream about white tulips, it means we are entering a new experience, a fresh start or a new beginning. Pink tulips offer congratulations.

Blue tulips are rare. They represent uniqueness and individuality. We saw no blue tulips at the national shine prayer gardens.

Tulips have amazing colors. They ooze out simplicity. Walking with God in the tulip garden reminds us to stop burdening our souls with meaningless busywork. We complicate our faith by obsessing about doctrine or denominations, worn out belief systems, and controlling institutional policies.

Daisies Represent Original Innocence

Daisies represent purity, love, and innocence. My daughter reminded me that she gave her beloved and departed mom daisies. Her mother would say "ups-a daisy" when encouraging Linda to get up when she fell down. Wordsworth and Shakespeare used a daisy chain in Hamlet to represent Ophelia's innocence. The praise and admiration of daisies was the theme of his poem "To the Daisy." Daisies can be eaten. They are a common addition to salads. They are the April birth month flower.

The focus of the daisy is the bright yellow center surrounded by white petals. It can be likened to the sun radiating in every direction. Daises remind us of Jesus words: "The eye is the lamp of the body. If your eye is healthy, your whole body will be full of light; but if your eye is unhealthy, your whole body will be full of darkness." Matthew 6:22-23. How we see the world determines not only what we see but how we respond.

The abundant array of flowers in the shine prayer gardens gave us a sense of awe and reverence. The Spirit whispers encouragement to us from the flowers that move us toward our own blossoming. In Nebraska the crocus with its persistent blooming peeks its head through the snow and ice from under hard rocks. We get discouraged and we shrink from the difficult and painful. There is light at the end of life's tunnels, but the way through them is through darkness.

Saints speak of "the dark night" as a container for transformation. Darkness in life's cocoons serve to incubate the growth of the butterfly. Tough times can be used as rich soil for growing our souls.

After a baccalaureate high school message in 1998 at a Lutheran Christian High School, I closed the worship celebration sermon with this prayer.

"Joyous God of the impossible, when I am too restless to pray, let me rest in your unconditional mercy. Let me rely on Jesus as your living Word and on your Spirit that ever intercedes. Let me learn from Scripture and be lifted by the prayers of your people. Make my life a prayer as I seek to do justice, love kindness, and walk humbly with you. Even when prayers seem impossible, I know that nothing is impossible for you. Amen."

Chapter Four

Soil for The Soul

Most of Jesus' ministry was with rural people. As he taught, he used images that had to do with growing plants and crops. He spoke of vineyards and wine. He talked about soil and seed, weeds and labor, fertilizing and pruning, and ultimately the harvest.

Every garden begins with the soil. Jesus told in a parable about a man who sowed seed. Some of the seed grew and produced abundant fruit. Other seeds did not. Jesus said the soil made the difference. The sed can be perfect, but if it is not sown in good soil, it will of little use. The problem is not with the seed.

Life is like that. God gives us talents, potential, and gifts. If the life soil is filled with toxins such as shame, bitterness, and arrogance, there will be no growth. Humans were created in the image of God. The problem is the soil. We need to examine the soil. A soil examiner looks at the soil each year to make suggestions. Farmers declare that there is a difference between soil and dirt. Dirt is inert. Dirt is composed of sand, debris, broken rock, and stuff without organic material. Dirt by itself will not bring life.

Manure matters to the soil.

Those who are not farmers or gardeners cannot understand why manure matters so much in fertile soil.

Dumping a load of manure on your land seems vile, even putrid.

There are seasons in our lives when our situation stinks the most. One thing we learn from tending the soil is that the most difficult and ugly days of our lives create the desired environment for ravishing growth. God allows the hard times to act as fertilizer in the garden of our souls.

When life throws something with an undesired odor, we can plant another crop of joy and let it thrive. When disappointment raises an unforgettable odor, we can sow a future crop of hope despite the smell.

Manure boosts the growth in a garden. Difficult people, rancid events, and putrid circumstances in life promotes something beautiful in us. What the enemy meant for evil in our lives has been used to make us whole and lovely. Manure acts as a highest-powered growth stimulant in soil. God walks with us when fetid conditions arrive in our pathway. God is more than able to bring a bumper crop of rapid growth in spite of the smells. The odor itself is joy. James 1:2-4.

We are not buried. We have been planted. The soul inside of us holds a seed of joy. Let joy radiate from the smell despite the darkness. Peace that passes understanding will help us stand up to anything.

Soil is what is needed. Its organic material makes things grow. The word soul comes from the Latin language as humus. Soil teems with life. Many pastors mark the foreheads of the community with ash as a reminder that we are mortal. Humans come from humus. To humus, we return when we are no longer living.

Composting is done in Nebraska. They take food waste and lawn waste, place it in a barrel with a little topsoil and turn it often, and you have good topsoil. The image is of dead stuff turning into life-giving soil. Winemakers talk much about soil. Taste of place is a term about composition of the soil and the atmosphere of a place for the process of making wine. The best wines have been stressed. When stressed, the vines sink their roots deeper seeking out the moisture and needed nutrients. Psalm 1 uses the expression about a tree that grows by sinking roots into the soil.

Imagine God sampling your wine. God swirls it around in the glass. God holds it up to the light. Breathing deeply, God might say, "This is good stuff. You held on when times were tough. You never broke away or quit but stayed connected. You refused to be satisfied with shallow answers. Well done, good and faithful servant.

What are we planting in our gardens of life? Life is like a garden. What is growing in our lives is what we have planted? Plant the seeds you want to grow and tend them. Like a well-tended garden, what we focus on is what grows. We are the master gardeners of our lives.

Numerous writers have attempted to define "soul." John Ortberg wrote *Soul Keeping* about the health of the soul. He helps us recover the connection to God. His book brings insight into what the soul is and its relevance as one of the most mysterious and neglected topics. He wrote that the soul is real life. It is what God breathed into humankind. God gives us tools to care for the soul.

"What shall it profit a man, if he shall gain the whole world, and lose his own soul? Or what shall a man give in exchange for his soul?" Mark 8:36-37, KJV. Most writers I have read agree that the soul is what integrates your will, your mind, and your relationships into a single, entire living being. The psalmist wrote, "Bless the Lord, O my soul; and all that is within me. Psalm 103:1, KJV.

The soil may reveal that our flowers and plants are drooping. Petals and leaves become yellow or burnt brown, limp and sickly. This happens when we place them inside a bushel basket or a pot. The plants may need fresh air. Inside a pot the soil becomes stale. Confinement is just too tight. We need to expand the container or to repot. Perhaps in our lives, it is easier to stay in the familiar pot. We must seek new outlets for the growing inner spirit. Being repotted requires patience. We must continue to adjust in new containers. That is what plants and flowers do.

The flourishing soul receives life from outside to create energy and vitality within and receives blessing beyond itself. Read Ephesians 2:10, John 7:37-39. We are humans from the humus, soil with a soul. Humans are a mysterious combination of the breath of God and the dust of the earth. Our connection with the soil means we are part of all creation. Every living thing has common roots. Humans are related to every living thing. In the second creation account in Genesis, humans are created first, then plants, and then animals. We are not machines with a soul. We are soil with a soul. The flourishing soul needs to maintain a connection with the soil of promise. Walking with God in the woods, hiking in the mountains, and quietly moving along a beach will clear our vision. If we love every flower, each plant, all animals, and ourselves, we will know the mystery of *jouissance* and why God so loved the world.

When we grow up, we tend to re-create the emotional and spiritual environment of our early family home lives. His is true as we pass on our tending to sin in all of our ancestors. We are all victims of victims. If your mother did not know how to love herself, or your father could not love himself, they could never teach us to love ourselves. They did the best they could with their own experiences during their own childhood.

God blesses humankind immediately after creating them. Genesis 1:26-28. Humans were made in the image of God. By highlighting maleness and femaleness of humans, the biblical narrative reveals the complementary diversity of persons who are human and different. Human beings are related, but not identical. God made us as social beings. We need mutually supportive relationships between diverse people.

The Nebraska and Midwest prairies reach their zenith in the summer. Watered by violent thunderstorms, millions of acres of grassland promise a new life. This past year, I drove throughout Nebraska to share my vision of joy. We can drive through these grasslands for hours without encountering another soul. The drive throws out all complexity from our souls. We hear no sound but the wind and the rustling of the grasses. Their tall plant heads sway with the breeze. The scent of the sagebrush fills the air. We are dazed by the colors in the wildflowers. Their plants grow as wild as the weeds. These annual wildflowers are fickle things. Unless they go to seed and find conditions through the winter acceptable, they will not germinate. Wildflowers are more reliable than annuals. Some are popular with gardeners as a result. Seedlings can be grown in a nursery. Cut back the faded flowers so they do not expand growth energy on seed production. Water is important. Mild fertilizer helps. No wonder the motto for Nebraska is "the good life."

God has given me the privilege to live my life teaching, preaching, and writing. I am grateful and in awe. People have sought my counsel as a pastor and a licensed psychotherapist. We are not always appreciated. Speaking comes naturally, but I am blessed to expressing myself in differing places. God and the saints, our departed loved ones, and the angels cheer for us as we live the reams God has had for us from the beginning. Those dreams are bigger than we can comprehend in the moment.

Life is about love. Loving God and loving people releases unlimited passion and energy. We shall one day be repotted into perfect soil.

Chapter Five

Sowing the Seed

Springtime is sowing time. Farming has changed from the past. Tractors are guided by GPS systems with sub-inch accuracy so that not one inch of the soil is missed. The rows are never overlapped. Seeds are precisely inserted into the prepared soil including a scientifically measured shot of insecticide to combat rootworm.

Growth begins with the sowing of seed. A seed is a tiny thing. A seed is an ordinary thing. Joy in our families and friends does not come if we fail to be grateful. A desirable harvest can not emerge from sowing bad seed. We tend to give up sowing spiritual seed because we feel our deeds are ordinary. They are unremarkable.

God told Adam that all living things increase by planting seeds. Genesis 1:29.

Apple trees cannot produce orange trees. Orange trees cannot produce apple trees. A seed has a genetic code inside to recreate a plant that it came from. The seed will multiply itself thousands of times if it is allowed to grow. When the seed brings forth its fruit, there are many more seeds inside that fruit.

Think about an orange or an apple. A healthy plant can multiple the numbers of the fruit. We start with a small seedling. That seed does not look like an apple or orange. If we did not know with trust the possible result, we would not believe it had become fruit. When the first tiny shoot comes up, we don't stomp on it and declare, "That's not a real plant." We might say, "Oh my joy, here it comes." It all comes from sowing one little seed.

Small and ordinary as a seed might be, as long as it is alive it will sprout. A tiny seed is faithful and reliable in doing what God meant it to do. Spiritual seed is faithful also. It produces good fruit in due season. Human beings need the same patience and trust in sowing to the spirit as the farmer has in sowing to the earth. "Behold the farmer waits for the precious produce of the soil, being patient about it, until it gets the early and late rains." James 5:7-8.

After the dormancy of winter, new growth springs into life. Birds return from their southern homes. Buds emerge on the trees as they discover again the warmth of the earth. Crocuses and other spring flowers begin to carpet the land as it throws off its winter coating. The creation opens to unexpected possibilities. Life shows itself in every corner of the world.

A few farmers still use horse-drawn planters. A few others plant crops by hand.

In Jesus day and in our day, the farmer's goal is to get the good seed into good soil. The seed would grow while it still has life in it. The seed is small but powerful. It produces fruit if conditions are right to achieve the intended purpose. Fields in Israel were small. They were separated from one another by paths that became like concrete from the throngs of people and animals walking on them. Any seed that hit this hard ground would lie there until the birds gobbled it up. Jesus saw the land was as solid rock with just a thin layer of soil. The sun would bake the rock, which kept the soil hot, causing the seed to germinate quickly. Without a root system, the plants withered and died.

Other seed was strangled by thistles and thorns and produced no produce. It is impossible to grow a healthy garden when it is filled with weeds. Seeds of weeds are endemic to the soil.

Weeds are the source of poison in our gardens. Unforgiveness is a poisoned weed. My grandmother had a plague on her living room wall that read, "Resentment hurts the vessel in which it is stored more than the object on which it is poured." Chronic anger and resentment are toxic to the soul. Unforgiveness is a mighty rock to remove during the inner journey. Forgiveness is not condoning. We forgive people. We do not forgive bad behavior. Forgiveness is letting go of the toxic poison. Toxic feelings do their dirty work, and we have lost our souls and profited absolutely nothing. Mark Twain said, "Forgiveness is the fragrance that the violet sheds on the heel that has crushed it."

The hymn "In the Garden" sticks in my head. Walking with God and hearing God's voice in the garden is a giant step to unconditional forgiveness. It is demonstrating love through mercy. Because we are connected, when we harm somebody else, we are in fact hurting ourselves. Revenge harms another person, and it is a form of violence. With violence comes counterviolence. More violence is generated.

Jesus said the good ground was not hard, hindered, or hollowed. A Jewish farmer who had a rich harvest was seven times what was sown. A miracle crop had yields of sixty or a hundred times.

Seeds explain living beyond this life. The parable of the sower tells us about successful sowing of seeds. The seedbed of the soul or the soil is important to the survival of the seed. Nebraska farmers cover the soil with a layer of organic dirt twice the diameter of the seed. Covering the seed with heavy soil will cause the seed to struggle to break through the ground. Lightweight seed covering soil is needed instead of simple garden earth. Sterilized steer manure, compost, leaf mold, or peat moss are possible. Press a seed gently with the hand to prevent washout. Sprinkle with water. Sowers will benefit from the soft and rich seedbed. Ralph Waldo Emerson said, "When I go into my garden with a spade, and dig a bed, I feel such an exhilaration and health that I discover I have been defrauding myself in letting others do for me what I should have done with my own hands."

As we digest the meaning of the parable of the sower, most times we focus on the soil types and the heartedness of the seeds. Focus on the fertile soil, the stones, and the weeds. How do we feel about the gardener? Get together with a prayer partner or family friend or your house church. Focus on the gardener sowing seeds. Ask your significant other, "When do you think about the gardener, what do you ponder? What words come to you in describing the sower?" Those few gathered in the Spirit of Joy Church in Nebraska shared their thoughts. Those gardeners appear to be foolish. Some said they thought the sower was wasteful. Why did the sower waste good seed on rocky soil? Sowing those seeds among weeds obviously would overwhelm the small seeds. Sowing the seeds for all of tomorrow's flowers and fruit are inside the seeds of today.

As we flip the image, we might think of the time we were on rocky ground. Think of divorce, unemployment, failure, or a disappointment. Continue to focus on the image of thorns and weeds. God keeps sowing seeds into our barren thorny souls. When we refused to walk with God, God continues to shower us with acceptance and love. We must cultivate an attitude of gratitude as we wait for the thorns to die and decompose. We wait for the spring rain to arrive. God will walk beside each gardener as we help others grow in faith. Flowers and plants give us oxygen for our lungs and for our souls. Slow down and sit in the garden, gazing upon its beauty that cannot gaze upon itself.

Soil, soul, and spirit feed us. The parables of Jesus are filled with images of fields and flowers, planting and plowing, the soil and fertile plains. Jesus touched upon the creative force that is the kingdom growing inside of us. Sowing seeds of joy come with every spade of soil. Gardeners sense that our garden and life is changing. As the vegetables mature, so does the soul. We plant seeds of hope and resurrection. We share the bounty of the garden with others. We rake away hurts and habits We water the green plants with gratitude and enjoy the showers of blessings. We can pull the resisting weeds that choke our progress. To get something you never had, you have to do something you never did.

Planting a seed is the simple act of getting something into motion to create the life wanted and longed to happen. Planting a whole garden is daunting and full of anxiety. Plant seeds that you never planted. Do it even if it involves just one seed. Take care of tending to your little seedling. To get something you never had. A leafy green thing will greet you. Nothing is more exciting than seeing your seed turn into something that blooms. When cared for with nourishing soil, rays of sunlight and water changes that seed and it becomes what it was meant to be. To realize positive change, let go of the past. Embrace the new thing that has never been.

Seeds need time to grow.

A garden is not created over a night. Focus on the positive. Something new forms from the earth. A seed must change if it is to grow. No seed can remain to be a seed forever. Seeds bring something we never had. We have an appetite for instant gratification leading us further away from what God wants for us. A life without patience and self-discipline leads to ruin. Farmers can't buy a box of self-control to satisfy our appetites, tempers, and impulses. These non-productive habits have been chosen by us. Our human souls are delicate compositions of body, mind, and spirit. We have instincts and we are capable of conditioned responses.

When a seed flowers, every person will recognize its beauty. After a seed undergoes a transformation and takes on a new form, everyone appreciates it for what it has to offer. Every seed has something new, something more to contribute. Go out to the garden and start planting seeds. With a little time, patience, and work, what appears to be an empty plot of dirt will be filled with beauty and growth. Discipline makes us free. Free will does not stifle us. We will with the strength of the joy of God to give back in love and service. Free will can indicate that we choose to think of our lives wasting in selfish pursuit of shallow, superficial, and demeaning things. We live in a world of complex and unlimited opportunity. God has a vision for each life.

The happiest people I know hold a sense of mission. They ooze out a joy that nothing can take away. These people have come to believe that they are suited to the task and they have the conviction that they are called. Their joy is independent of circumstances. Their purpose is higher than their gratification.

Visualizing and realizing our journey's purpose is both simple and complicated. We are asked to start now and to wait patiently. It is simple because the needs of other people are self-evident. Our ability to help them is enormous. That ability is complicated because there is so much need and we cannot attend to all of it. We are living in fear because we do not know how this will work out, but God will help us work it out to completion. We must learn to enjoy uncertainty. Being uncertain is the sign that all is well. God will care about the details.

Begin immediately to do what you can with what you have, wherever you find yourself. Focus on what you came to live on earth to give. Your unique mission will be revealed. God speaks to us in silence. Slow down. Listen. Inner calm and a desire to serve will come as we walk with God.

Human vanity is best served by a reminder that, whatever our accomplishments, sophistication, artistic pretention, we owe our existence to a six-inch layer of topsoil. And to the fact that the rains come. There are many things hiding in our mud puddles after a rain. We panic when faced with change. We can never control every outcome. Old patterns will surface. Calm down. Be freed of self-entrapment.

Guilt is called the mafia of the mind. Guilt happens when what we think we should do or become is in opposition to what we are. Those shameful patterns cannot survive in an environment of support and light.

Celebrate the blossoming soul. Give yourself a reward for having the courage to face the mud following the rain when we do the "dirty work" so to speak. We reap the benefits from this spiritual journey. We gain godly wisdom and joy that nobody outside of you will ever understand. Those people who do not choose to get their hands in the mud will not be supportive of us.

The soil we plant in is our subconscious mind. The seed is a new affirmation. A whole new experience is in a tiny seed. We water our souls with affirmations. We let the sunshine of positive thoughts beam. When we weed the garden, we pull out the negative thoughts that come up. And when we see the smallest evidence, we can't hold back our joy.

Seeds are a miracle of life. They point to what is possible. Seeds speak to the abundance that God intends for all creation. Every seed we sow in gardens and fields are meant for blessing. The seeds we sow in acts of compassion, peacemaking, healing, and justice, small as they are, like a mustard seed, are a source of blessing. The seed we sow are intended to produce a harvest far beyond the tiny seed we begin with in our garden. Reflect on the seed we grow and the impact of a seed. During worship in the Spirit of Joy Church, we gave each person a handful of seeds. We asked the congregation to place the seed in a container of earthly soil placed in the center. Each person was invited to offer words about how they can care for the land that receives the seeds. Finally, each gave words on how they might sow seeds of action to bless the world around them. We ended by praying that we would learn to walk gently on the earth and preserve it for future generations.

When we sow seeds into the soil of the ground, we expect something back out of the earth. A seed does not become another seed. It becomes something much more. When our souls are germinated by God's spirit, they become something bigger. Without God our souls wither and die. Without the ability to reproduce, the fruit that God created in Eden would have disappeared.

Saint Francis of Assisi, or Francesco di Pietro Giovanni di Benardo, lived from 1181 to 1226. Thinking of sowing seeds could not be complete without Saint Francis' prayer, "Make Me an Instrument of Thy Peace."

Lord, make me
an instrument
of thy peace,
Where there is
hatred, let me
sow love:
Where there is injury, pardon:
Where there is doubt, faith:
Where there is despair, hope:
Where there is darkness, light:
Where there is sadness joy.

O divine Master, grant that I may be not so much seek
To be consoled as to console,
To be understood as to understand,
To be loved as to love,
For it is in giving that we receive.
It is in pardoning that we are pardoned.
It is in dying to self that we are born to eternal life.

Chapter Six

Sowing and Reaping

Sowing and reaping is a perfect analogy of life. No other expression is clearer than to see life as a process of sowing seed and reaping a harvest. We are reaping what we sowed and sowing what we shall reap. Thoughts and actions are seeds being sown for a future harvest.

When a gardener says that which we sow we shall reap does not apply to those lovely pictures on the front of seed packages. Note that farming and gardening are the slowest of performing arts.

Sowing and reaping express an analogy of life. Every person living on earth are now reaping what was sown. Nebraska farmers know well that they sow with patience. James 5:7-8 speaks to them and us. With just a handful of seed, there is the potential to feed the family for a season. Our family enjoys sweet corn all year from our annual work of "putting up corn."

Figurative seed demands faith and patience. Today a few words, thoughts, decisions, and actions, have the potential to affect the future. John 4:36-38 indicates that each of us working farms and gardens today will sow what another reaps. Whenever we receive an inheritance knows what this means. A little child dies of Covid-19 or of AIDS. The child may have reaped what another sowed.

Jeremiah 12:13 says, "They have sown wheat and reaped thorns." We might sow seeds that are spoiled. Good seed was sown in your garden dwelling, but bad seed might grow. Hosea 8:7 says, "They sow the wind, and reap the whirlwind. The grain stalk has no head. It will yield no flour. Even if it were to yield, strangers would devour it." Goodness can overwhelm the whirlwind. We may reap more than we thought from the seed we sow.

Paul wrote that we reap what we sow. Read Galatians 6:7-8. If we sow evil, we reap evil. Seed can only produce its own kind. Paul tells us that we can never sow to the flesh and reap from the spirit. The seed is not the harvest reaped. A farmer, a gardener, or flower grower will reap sparingly if they sow sparingly. See II Corinthians 9:6. The more joyfully we sow, the more joy we will reap.

Sowing and reaping are agricultural terms. Farmers and gardeners depend on this principle in the natural realm. Never be deceived into thinking you can sow bad seed, and nothing will happen. When a farmer plants corn, he will reap corn. If a gardener sows tomato seed, tomatoes will be the result.

When we sow in the flesh, we reap corruption. The genetic code of our flesh has the potential for producing corruption. Soul-filling action results in eternal life. Life is built into our genetic code because God is the creator of life.

If we need soul-changes in our living, we cannot begin by trying to reap a different harvest. Human beings must sow a different seed. We sow what we expect but hope for a differing harvest. What does the Bible reveal about sowing to the Spirit? In Galatians Paul says to look at the fruit of the Spirit: love, joy, peace, patience, kindness, goodness, faithfulness, gentleness, and self-control. Fruit is produced by sowing the seeds of that fruit. We ask God to help us sow these in our life gardens. Every choice we make is important. Small choices accumulate during a lifetime, showing up in our character. Character develops one decision at a time. When we lie, we become a liar. When we choose to steal, we become a thief. If we choose to be patient, we become patient. When we choose to do loving things, we become a loving person.

If we are not living in the Spirit, the problem is not God. Sin will always seep into our lives, but we are no longer a slave to sin. We are no longer a slave to anger. We are not slaves to immorality, impatience, or greed. Transformation and obedience do not come in one big leap. Small seeds keep us from being paralyzed in guilt. Walking with God in a new Garden of Eden results in touching lives all around us. Quiet daily decisions and seeking God's ways brings more joy than we can imagine.

Our calling is not to know how God will use us, but to simply and humbly sow in the Spirit, and ask God for us to bear godly fruit through our lives.

Reaping comes in a different time than when we sow. There is a delay time between sowing and reaping. The flesh continues to tell us to sow what we want. God speaks to our souls in faith as we sow good seed, but we are not experiencing the reaping. Do not grow weary, in due season we will reap if we do not quit. God is kind and loving to give us the passion and the courage to see and seize opportunities to do good in the lives of others. God is calling us out of our comfort zones and to "comfort ye, comfort ye my people."

Sowing in Tears, Reaping in Joy

Life is a climb, a journey. We are pilgrims. Read Psalm 126. The pilgrim in this Psalm is walking through a sad time. This psalmist remembers with joy a time when God restored the fortunes of Israel. It was like a dream. The writer longs to live it all again.

We may go out weeping today, sowing our tearful seeds, but there is a harvest of joy we shall reap for all eternity. Perhaps you remember a time in your life journey when you were filled with the joy described in Psalm 126:2. Our living videos also record the sorrows as told in verses five and six. What has God done to assure us that our destiny is one filled with eternal joy?

Perhaps we read Psalm 126 with heavy hearts. It tests the boundaries of our faith.
The joys of heaven are far more spectacular than what is living in this world.

Survivors of the Babylonian captivity felt like resurrecting from the dead as they made their way back to Jerusalem. The exile was a season of reaping.
Miraculously, God brought a harvest of new life for the people. Let us not grow weary of doing good, for in due season, we will reap, if we do not give up. As we pray in the Garden, we can ask for the stamina to continue to sow seeds of obedience and witness.

If you want fresh tomatoes, plant tomato seeds. Nobody would plant hemlock seeds and then wonder what a poisonous plant is doing in the garden. Ask yourself what you want. Plant the seeds that will give you those results. Gardens and farms need favorable conditions. Assess the climate and temperature, the amount of sun light, available water, exposure to wind, the PH levels of your soil. As you visualize your life, set goals with your weaknesses and strengths, your likes and dislikes, character and temperament, and your choice of people to hang out in mutually satisfying places. Build a fence around your garden so it will be pest free. The last thing you want is for deer, rabbits, and furry animals munching away.

Enjoying reaping a bountiful crop is soul satisfying. If your harvest was not as good as expected, if your plants failed to bear fruit, analyze what went wrong. Try again. There is no such thing as the end to the bounty of earth. There will be enough for everybody. That's what we learn in the garden. If we give plants all that they need, they will more in return. Audrey Hepburn enjoyed gardening. She said, "To plant a garden is to believe in tomorrow."

In the doing of these good actions, we find hope for those past seeds we repent from doing. Every person alive today has sown to the flesh. Joy comes as we focus on love. We must never want to use the sovereignty of God as an excuse for continual disobedience to God. Joy comes as a balm for our souls when we consider sowing to the flesh with regret as we repent.

Focusing on the good and being grateful is the quickest way out of negativity, stinking thinking, and overlooking the solutions. To focus on our blessings, we amplify them. Focusing on our failures and struggles also amplifies them. Never estimate the power of gratitude to empower us. Whatever worldly weeds grow into life, focus on the good and good will grow. God wants to walk with us as a conscious gardener who tends the crops, waters the flowers, arranges the rocks of life.

As God makes it clear on how we are given the power to change, we will not wait to eradicate our fears. When we face our fears, the shadows become weaker. "Fear not," Jesus often said. We can sidestep our growing pains coming from painful experiences. God has made earth like a large garden. God has asked each one of us to be a gardener and to help keep it healthy and growing.

The ancient people of Israel knew that property ownership was long-term. Farmers in Nebraska value their land so much, they will not sell a foot. In Israel the extraordinarily varied topography and climate encouraged long term tenure. The uneven highland terrain produces irregular wind and rainfall patterns. Diverse ecological niches exist in close proximity. A farm could sit partially in the rain shadow of a hill or mountain. They received less rainfall than a neighboring farm. Growing the most possible and quality crops on one farm would require different techniques and strategies than those required for the farm next door.

Farmers rely on diversified crops for nutritional balance. This is a hedge against natural disasters. Farmers create a staggered schedule of planting and harvesting to ensure a steady food supply throughout the year. This schedule provided limited protection against uncertain rain, plant disease, and pestilence. If one crop failed, the farmer could fall back on other crops harvested at different times. A clan of farmers shared labor for common tasks such as building and maintaining terraces. They offered mutual assistance when crops failed, and they banded together for any necessary sharing. The clans had a strong sense of solidarity, reinforced by a culture of shame and honor. Those cut off from family or land experienced a crisis of personal identity.

Job was cut off from family past and future, from his property. His whole life was utterly ruined. He had lost his personal identity. His physical condition mirrored his social condition. His skin became porous. We know skin protects our individuality. It is a sense organ. Job held anxiety, fear, buried gunk, and he realized he was being threatened. His sores came from his unexpressed anger that had settled in. He became a non-person lacking family, property, or connection to God.

The soul wants to blossom. We prepare our plots of land for plants. That same kind of preparation is required. Clear the inner garden of debris and weeds. We must set aside the stones before the fruit of the Spirit can flourish. Inner space opens up. Healthy air sets in. Sunlight is now free. Pick up the spade. Get your sharpened hoe. The time is perfect for our souls to burst forth in beauty and joy.

Seeking to follow Jesus in our age, we live with a growing population. We must be mindful of all creatures great and small. There have been vast changes to the earth since the time of Jesus. Humanity has shifted from an agricultural base to an industrial foundation. Burning of fossil fuels pumps tons of greenhouse gases into the atmosphere. For decades scientists have warned that pollutants cause climate change. The message of Good News and the hope for a new Garden of Eden includes tending to the environment. That is what celebrating Earth Day is about. It concerns the fragility of the garden God planted and our responsibility to care for it, as it is written in Genesis. God gave Adam and Eve the mandate to care for God's glorious garden and that command has passed to us. As we choose to walk with God in the bounteous garden, may we each take with us a renewed commitment to serve as God's gardeners. A garden offers itself to the light and does not control. Roses turn into roses. Cucumbers turn into cucumbers.

Our souls can be shaped into what they were meant to be. Trust God in the silence.

Weed it and reap.

Chapter Seven

Pulling Weeds and Pruning Roses

Pulling weeds is vital to gardening. Digging them out while they are small causes the least disruption to the vegetables and fruits and flowers. Pulling weeds keeps weeds from stealing the water, sunshine, and the soil. Any kind of change is disruptive. Pruning and pulling out weeds is necessary for the healthy growth. Become a skilled pruner in your own garden, and you will understand the pruning process that occurs between God and your soul.

There was a plague in a farmer's lawn that read, "In a garden full of weeds dare to be a flower."

Good gardens do not just naturally grow. Weeds do. I have felt my back ache from weeding my plot of turf. Pulling weeds is the story of life. That soil in our soul is most valuable. Jesus taught that spiritual fruitfulness or barrenness depended on the quality of the soil that receiving the seed. Pesky weeds squeeze the life out of fruit-producing seedlings.

Worry and anxiety are the weeds that draw us in differing directions. Our busyness crowds out the best. We have become occupied with how to please other people. We achieve and perform to find significance. On our life journey, we sever the taproot of the weeds of distraction. The deceitfulness of riches is seen in the poverty of the world. The 99 per cent are just existing.

The veneer of the one per cent's prosperity disguises the hopelessness in the earth. Wealth is a deceptive weed that chokes out our responsiveness to God. Be aware of the prosperous times. In days of recession or depression, we try to play it safe and risk nothing for God. The garden that needs weeding is our desires or passionate craving such as sexual lust or other perversions. Any desire that drives us, controls our thinking, or preoccupies our minds is a weed that can destroy us.

Weeds have potential for multiplication. We break off the stem of the dandelion and observe the seeds flying. The blowing wind launched tiny, angel hair seeds. How many dandelions are in one seed-ball? If gardeners let one weed grow in in the soil, it can result in a crop failure. All soil has weeds. And our lives. Ask God to walk with you in the cool of your garden. God will do fresh cultivation in the soil of your soul.

The world is a better place because you lived. Tend your garden so as to feed, in body and soul, all who come into your circle. Cultivate yourself to become a garden of abundant life. John Wesley once wrote: "Do all the good you can by all means you can, in all ways you can, in all places you can, at all the times you can, to all the people you can, as long as you can."

Not all plants need pruning. If the gardener wants to maximize the edible parts of certain plants, judicious pruning goes a long way. Unlike harmful habits that crowd us and must be weeded away, pruning is done to the plant itself to encourage growth. Pruning is painful. We can trust God the Gardener with the pruning shears.

When my daughter Linda would see her parents pruning, she wondered if the plants and trees felt pain or relief from pruning them in the winter. If they are not properly pruned, some branches grow too close to the others causing tree sores and inviting disease. Fruit will not continue to flourish from a diseased tree. That's how it is with growth and life. Thomas Wolfe wrote, "One is nearer God's heart in a garden than anywhere else on earth." That personal secret garden is where souls preside. Gardens of any type require the initial planting of the seed. The mystery stirs and the seed gives birth to a sprout. This is a necessary process that leads all living things the joy of being.

Every living thing is imbued with goodness because God created everything and called it "very good." As a gardener pulls weeds, she or he realizes that these weedy plants once contributed to the diet and health of people in past times. Ralph Waldo Emerson wrote: "What is a weed? A plant where virtues have not yet been discovered." As winter seed sprouts to life, we find little good in the abundance of weeds. Pulling weed is best done after or during a rain. Then the soil is so soft the roots find nothing to test a gentle tug. Strive to take out the entire taproot of a weed such as dandelions. The work completed in removing these weeds pays off later in the year.

Pruning roses is an example of life. The gardener knows we have to prune modern roses. Most roses are pruned during winter. The flowering is finished. Growth is at a standstill. An older woman had an unkempt garden in front of her home. She had pale and distressed hybrid roses. She has recovered from Covid-19. She mentioned wanting to prune her rose bushes. Her roses were thorny and tangled with long, spindly branches poking out. I ask her if I could offer help. I told her that I enjoyed planting and pruning roses. She finally said, "I am grateful for your help."

She had 14 overgrown rose bushes. I placed the cuttings in a heap. This work took a whole afternoon as I used a pair of old secateurs. Large-jawed long handed ones work much better. I persisted and I completed the job. As light and air gets to the center of the plant, it will resist fungal disease. The roses could now breathe a breath of fresh air.

People are like those roses. We develop concepts and beliefs that are negative to our human development. These need to be pruned away. Just like a rose bush, we resist. My ministry is about pruning people not plants. People resist when we attempt to relieve them of the weight of old, non-productive growth. People cling to outmoded beliefs with the tenacity of an addict. Just as a flower becomes compressed and distorted with the weight of those gnarled branches, people become depressed with the unproductive weight that brings growth to a standstill.

Walking in a Garden of Eden teaches life lessons. In the garden there is the effort to be present. Each flower is fleeting. That's why each one is special. There is always more work to be done in the garden. Nothing is more important than taking time for enjoying it without judgment. Smell the flower. Touch the flower. Remember when the flower was first planted. Even in happy times, we feel overwhelmed. I feel it as I step outside into the garden. With prayer, I refuse to let this draining energy put me into a state of indecision. When life piles the stress upon us, we just cannot comprehend the end of the tunnel.

All of us have experienced those times when the future appears empty. Depression is a way of life. It does not have to be an endless struggle. We live on an earth filled with darkness. God desires our walking in the garden when we cannot see Light at the end of the tunnel. Jesus called himself the Light of the world. Walking with Jesus means we do not have to choose to live in darkness. Read John 8:12, II Corinthians 4:6. The world is darkened. The tunnel appears darker. We have experienced record cold and record snow. The global pandemic with Covid-19 has killed millions around the world. Being Christian does not give protection from the problems. Choose the Light of Christ. God has a plan to bring humankind back to walk with God. The Garden of God sings with the winds of winter. Winter carrots slowly set down their tender, promising roots in winter. The scarlet rosehips are fiery in winter.

We have been told that we need to self-isolate to hide from the risk of infection. Some are having to be alone for the first time. We are not alone wherever we are. In Christ, we are one body together. Those who possess and know how to use a computer can keep in touch and ask for help. Worship is best streamed live. God is mindful of those in isolation and in loneliness.

Fear is common as we make decisions in difficult times. The gospel of John assures us that there is no fear in love. The disciples of Jesus were terrified when they saw him walking on water. Jesus told them that what they were viewing is himself walking. He told them not to be afraid.

God is walking with us when we listen to the news that the whole world is in lock-down. Front-line workers work with the sick. God is working with each one. Paul assures us that God will cause all things to ultimately work for the good. Most of us will never understand. People will use their gifts and acts of kindness to support others. Strangers now pass each other on the streets. They smile as we acknowledge each other and walk with God in a community. Some people keep serving others motivated by compassion. They want nothing in return. The joy of the Lord is our strength. Read Psalm 28:6. Walking with God will enable us to outshine any darkness. Our hearts will leap in joy.

Seeds grow inside our souls in the darkness. God whispers invitations to our souls. We have to still our souls to notice the subtle messages. Dashing from one thing to another, we lose the rhythm of the growing garden. All of us are on a spiritual soul journey. We are not so much human beings on a spiritual journey, but we are spiritual beings on a human journey. As we become aware of our gentle flowering, we encourage the blossoming of other souls. Early spring brings life to bulbs hidden deep in the soil. Souls have bulbs of possibility.

In the mountains in North Carolina, there are many tunnels dug into the earth for cars and trains to have a more convenient journey. If you have never walked or drove through one, it can bring fear. Finally, we drive or walk along the sides of the tunnel. We see the light at the end of the tunnel. A tunnel can be a metaphor for circumstances or problems that surround us. We feel trapped and confined. We feel hopeless and anxious. Seeing the end of the tunnel light, we find ourselves back on the right track.

Weeding Other People's Gardens

We tend to want to weed other people's gardens. Spiritually speaking we perceive other people's responsibility by harboring resentment. We resent our bosses, our parents, violence and anger. We notice the specks in other people but fail the log in our own eyes. It is the utmost foolishness to shift the blame from others to ourselves or to God. Our attitude must be that no one is to blame, and everybody is responsible. That means we are to clear the air of finger-pointing.

The garden of our souls gets crowded and choked. The weeds of distractions clutter the way. Doubts are like dark clouds. We become as a flower bed with unwelcome weeds. Life brings upsetting apple carts. The furnace fails in the freezing winter. Our cars break down, the church closes, and family becomes sick. Life is as it is. With our small courage there are weeds of fear. The earth is filled with weeds. Our life journey is like a wild meadow. Pull the weeds if you can. Keep sowing seeds of faith. Acceptance of the weediness of the garden of the soul is part of the deal. There will come a final harvest.

A bouquet of weeds.

When my daughter was a little girl, she had a smudge of dirt on her face and a sparkle in her blue eyes. Her hands were behind her back. She came into our house through the basement stairs. She did not speak a word. Her impish grin spread irresistibly as she gave her mother a bouquet of weeds. Nancy immediately placed the "flower" in a lovely vase. These lovely plants graced the kitchen table for several days. There was loving gratitude for this thoughtful gift.

God will come to us as we give him our weeds. Everything God made was "very good." God treasures any gift, even weeds. Anything we give to our Father would be callow and cheap compared to what God has so generously given to us. Every time we give God all that we are, God throws her arms around us.

Offering our weeds to the Lover of Our Souls as a sacrifice of praise creates a sweet-smelling bouquet in the palace of eternity.

The thistle is the national flower of Scotland. Legend says that when the English were about to sneak up on the Scottish clans, the soldiers from England screamed out when the purple thistles pierced their skin. During one of my trips to Scotland, I purchased a beautiful necklace with a lovely purple thistle jewel in Nancy's favorite color.

In the eyes of God, the weed is as valuable as any flower. God and those who walk with attraction and love for wounded people sense this truth. They are compelled to talk with someone, to get to know them better, or to bring someone into their lives. Later we discover how unhappy they are living with unresolved trauma. If we do not do what they want, they will wound us.

God gave us an inborn temperament that thrives when we are helping to heal someone else. It hits us like a lightning bolt. We are drawn to give more attention to them. The spirit gave us confirmation of our diagnosis. A small laser focuses something inside of us. That inward activation is the beginning of our gearing up to help.

Most believe this is nonsensical. Getting entangled with others is our own fault. Others call us co-dependent. They say that we have no boundaries. We are in need of approval, and we never stand up for ourselves.

Chapter Eight

Living with *Jouissance* in the New Garden

Jouissance is a French word that means "deepest joy." *Jouissance* is a matter of deep joy, an assured security, living in the presence of God as if the kingdom of God had come. What does *jouissance* mean? To know it's meaning, I will tell you with a story.

When I was a young minister preaching in varied churches and wonderful places, our revival team at Carson-Newman often stayed in homes with gracious hosts from the community. People would offer so much for our comfort. During the All-South Bristol Crusade at Woodlawn Baptist Church, I stayed with my friend Richie Hagey and his family. They owned the local grocery store. Most of the time, I told the host that I just wanted simple food. When serving as a summer missionary in New Mexico, the associational missionary told us to eat whatever was placed in front of us. In many homes it was not a joy to taste what was prepared. Richie's mother told me that I could have whatever I wanted to eat.

The first morning, the hostess asked what she could serve me. I said, "Well, I'd like eggs, ham, a pancake with syrup, and biscuits and gravy." That was exactly what she prepared. The hostess went into her kitchen and enjoyed cooking. Now that was eating with *jouissance*.

And she and her family were delighted. Other members of our team said they had coffee or maybe cereal. Betty Manley said she wanted nothing to eat. Jimmy Temples drank a glass of orange juice and some cookies. Jesus told a parable in Matthew 22:1-14 about a king who arranged a wedding feast for his son. Nobody who was invited came to eat even with a fatted calf on the menu. The king then invited other people who might enjoy the feast. They experienced *jouissance*.

The word is more than good feelings or enjoying drinking and eating. Deepest joy, living in the presence of God, receiving an invitation to the fullness of life that God prepares for us. Joy is the foundation, the substructure that undergirds our living. When we refuse the sense of God's joy in us, even eating food becomes something we just have to do. The way we eat and our attitude towards mealtime may rob us of *jouissance*.

The ability for us to feel joy is like learning a new language. We are all born with this ability. Joy comes independent of everything else we experience. Some people still believe that joy is not innate. When we resist or deny the feelings of joy, life and relationships lose meaning. When we sense we are not living life fully, we lose touch with the intrinsic sense of joy. Joy restores and renews us.

Jouissance is good medicine.

Joy is good medicine. In Greece, hospitals were built near amphitheaters so patients could attend comedies to promote healing. In a well-known case, writer and peace promoter Norman Cousins was diagnosed with a life-threatening illness. He came to understand that negative feelings are detrimental to healing. Cousins watched humorous movies, read funny stories, and laughed his way back to wellness. Joy strengthens our immune systems. Joy boosts energy. Joy protects us from stress and exhaustion.

Locate a feeling of joy in your body. This could be perceived as a connection, well-being, happiness, peace, or any sensation. Feel the joy, and at the same time be aware of thoughts, emotions, or a situation that affects your body, mind, and soul. Open your eyes as you encourage the joy to accompany you as you enter your life.

These habits or practices have a deep resonance with the purposes of God and human constitution for human beings. They are pathways toward other elements of flourishing living. God has given each of us a personal invitation to a joyful and abundant life. Gratitude brings healing moments. Welcome thanksgiving for joy times in your body and mind. Take time to recall what you are thankful for in your mind, during walks with God or writing in a journal.

Joy is a gift from God. Paul reminded us, "May the God of hope fill you with all joy and peace through the power of the Holy Spirit." Romans 15:13.

Because joy is from God, anything that takes away joy is not from God. Joy becomes a standard of measure of our walking with God. If we allow our joy to be stolen by someone or something, that person or thing has become your bigger and most important god.

When we feel weak, and appear to have no strength left, the joy of the Lord will strengthen us. God's jouissance is based on the eternal promise of eternal life. Joy comes as prayers are answered. Read John 16:24. Joy is unconditional because it is based on the Word of God. Read Romans 14:17-18. Joy can be restored. See Psalm 51:12. When we sin, our joy can become unavailable. We are then filled with guilt. The overwhelming regret makes us feel separation from God until we accept forgiveness of our sins and again find the joy of our salvation. Joy is fulfilled in the presence of God. Joy begins with God. We have joys during our earth-bound journey. Full joy or my definition of *jouissance* will not happen until we are in God's presence. A bride and groom are happy months before the wedding. Both anticipate joy. Joy comes as we stay faithful to God.

With this joy we offer thanks for the seeds of promise. Bless these seed gifts for the service of all people. On earth day, we sing: "Thank you God for soil and air. Thank you, God for gardeners and farmers. Thank you, God, for making seeds grow. Thank you, God for the flowers."

Nothing can be more pleasant than the smell of dew and flowers and the sweet odor when the dew is on the roses. Joy is not a simplistic emotion. Associating joy with bright color, sunny days, and easy smiles can make it appear as straightforward and uncomplicated. Universities and divinity schools acted as if our weightier emotions merited scientific study and intensive reflection. A doctoral seminar on joy at Vanderbilt stimulated my life career as minister of joy to the world. Yale University Divinity School received a Templeton grant to study joy. For scholars heavy studies meant deep. Light became too shallow for serious study. Churches believed that a person who is joyful and full of cheer and bliss was less serious than one who is brooding and pensive. After more than 50 years, beginning at Vanderbilt and then at Yale, I discovered that while joy may be simple, it is not simplistic. In a garden, there are colorful flowers with roots extending down into the earth. Joy is light, but dark and deep illuminating. It is difficult to imagine something if you have not experienced it. If you have not viewed models of joy, you can find them now. Over the years I have collected thousands of people's description of their joy. These remind me of how joy is useful in differing life situations. People have shared that in a joy, they smile more, their shoulders relax, and worries are discarded. Their stories are stored on their life tapes that never slip by as they are aware of the signs of joyful moments. Joy filled people are less irritable and more approachable. Others confide in you. They are generous and less self-conscious. Joy unlocks these qualities.

It has been of unimaginable worth to see that joy is not an idle pursuit. I have struggled and found joy in life. Joy comes as a surprise. Humans cannot create it. Joy is dynamic, coming out of places we do not expect. The greatest struggles open up new space for joy. Struggles bring appreciation when it arrives. Be patient in waiting for joy to come back again. When we zoom out, looking at the bigger picture, we create an alignment between our aspirations for life and our activities. At the end of our journey on earth, we will hold no regrets.

Joy is a choice. It requires some changes. It might require a serious look at joy as your priority. Writing books about joy has been a wonderful transforming experience. It has involved numerous hours sitting at a desk. When a person makes joy a priority, we find a lens to reexamine how we are spending time, energy, and money. Only you can make it happen. The joy of the Lord is a deep mystery, an exquisite gift from God tucked into quiet corners and unexpected places.

Humans are not physically bound in chains. Even those living behind prison bars innately carry freedom. On this earth, our souls are in chains. Bound souls mean bound minds. Quietly we are being destroyed from the inside out. Signs of this lack of freedom are constant anger, agonizing grief, and paralyzing shame. Walking with Jesus in the garden, we find our bindings can be released. We are no longer shackled to negative emotions and thoughts. Why can we not let go of our pasts? Why do we fear living our lives?

God in Christ has unlocked our prison doors. God desires us to walk out of our cells. Perseverance and trust reveal the tools that God gave us to access freedom. The Word of God is living and active, sharper than a two-edge sword. Hebrews 4:12.

It is human nature to want to know joy and peace. Peace and joy are spiritual gifts. Peace and joy exist in the present moment. The moment we focus out of the moment, we cut off access to these spiritual gifts. Thank God for the journey of our soul, and for the body the soul resides in, for food, for shelter, for eyes that see, ears that hear, legs, arms, health, and love. Surrender to the wisdom of the Spirit. We are never alone. Joy is Jesus making sorrow sing.

It is our choice. God will guide us to live in alignment with our souls which is living in integrity with the highest good. We must be consistent. Moment by moment choose what brings you joy and peace.

Saint Teresa of Avila imagined an earthly journey filled with joy. She thought of God planting a garden within her. God asks us to water it and tend to the growth. She speaks of hauling water. We are to haul it bucket by bucket. The bucket is heavy with the weight of water. God points us in the direction where there is a water wheel. We keep at it with this gift of assistance. We smile as we see a stream of water flowing through the garden. And then it rains. Soon we just stand in the rain. This garden journey brings effortless joy.

We can continue to hoe and till our garden. We come to discover love that showers us like rain. This journey helps us focus on all the situations in our lives that are difficult to live with and accept. In *jouissance*, we enjoy standing in the rain of God's grace with faces lifted to the sky. We welcome life events that are uncomfortable. Fear and doubt are acknowledged, but these are not permanent in a life filled with creative adventure. Spirituality illumines our wellness in body, mind, and soul. To live in joy, we live life in complete emancipation. We feel the unconditional love of God as we become aware. Walking the path of joy, we come to realize that we are in God's presence. We receive divine protection. To be fixed in that assurance is to occupy a permanent place. Our spiritual being is the expression of eternal life. Life eternal is whole complete existence. Our inner beings are unfolded to realize the nature of life eternal before we enter into life as it is now. We are ascending into the freedom of God. We are becoming what the image of God in us promises. Our lives in every moment will be free, and that freedom will increase in perfect harmony with the soul's capacity for that freedom. As we grow in that freedom, we grow out of everything that is undesirable, adverse, or limiting.

There is no sickness in God. Human beings cannot be sick any more than light can be darkness. Our soul continues to be well and strong. The diseases and sickness that exist in the body now will disappear the moment we enter God's new Garden of Eden.

No separation exists in the spirit. Having the mind of Christ, we become conscious of divine oneness. We enter that mind when we walk in the presence of God.

With God in us, we are living the same life that God lives. Our personal life becomes the same expression as the life of God. Elements of disease, sickness, adverseness, imperfection, and darkness will disappear.

The joy of the Lord is our strength. We will realize that the strength of our Infinite Maker is our strength. The strength of God is limitless. In light of that truth, we cannot say we are not able to do anything. Nothing can cause us to be tired. Nothing will be too much for us. The flesh may now be weak. God's strength makes us strong.

Every part of our bodies, minds, and souls will live with limitless life. God lives an eternal, limitless life. That means that everything in life is formed, shaped, and developed by that power. We are fixed on high where everything created is in the image of God.

That word *jouissance* is special to me. I first heard it when I preached at the Emmanuel Baptist Church in Paris. Most French people use the word as common for intense pleasure, intellectual, spiritual, or sensual. The verb *jouir* means "to enjoy."

During the time following my sermon on joy, a French-speaking businessman from England thought of joy as something deep inside being relaxed. He felt calm, selfless, and happy. Cold dark clots dissolved in his soul.

A dark woman told us of her dream where vertical links were the color of a rosy flame that spanned from earth to the sky. It was in a garden as a center of connections where she knew no ego. A new self was released. The joy she felt was mystical.

Jouissance is defined as intense enjoyment. It is a release of the human tension of want or lacking. This joy brings the idea that our desires to find happiness as we do the will of God. Most people have admitted to not be committed to the passionate pursuit of joy.

What if the essence of disobeying God was the incapacity for supreme joy? What if this resulted in a loss of taste for what is supremely delicious? From the beginning of eternity God has been planning a kind of pleasure so great that eye has not seen, nor ear heard, nor has it entered humankind's imagination.
Discovering the roots by walking with God is so liberating. The world God created is still God-saturated on the ultimate path to become radiant with joy. Water is needed for all living things. Some cities have warm or smelly water to sooth thirst. Nebraska has more water underground than any other state. Our cold fresh tasting water is a *jouissance* for those who have never tasted such water.

Joy means to choose to live life through soul transformation. We experience the exultation of spirit. Joy frees us for acceptance of all that comes into life and refusing to permit them to color our lives. The *jouissance* compass steers us to find joy in family, friends, work, and everything. "Be joyful always." (I Thessalonians 5:16). Joy lives at the epicenter. Joy is the bright light that shines. Others see it in us as we reflect our passion and our calling. We smile more often. Smiles brighten our moods. Listen to God as God knows the path. It lures us out into nature to engage with plants, flowers, and wildlife. Imagine living on our own terms with nothing holding us back. *Jouissance* enables us to survive without sacrificing happiness. We will tend to think outside the box. We will solve problems in new ways.

The Greek word for joy is *chara*. This noun describes an inner gladness, delight, and rejoicing. Joy is a deep-seated pleasure based on spiritual realities. Joy is part of God's essence. The chorus from an old song describes joy: "Happiness happens, but joy abides. Remember it takes 74 muscles to frown, and 14 to smile." C.S. Lewis, the Oxford professor, came closer to *chara* when he expressed joy as an "unsatisfied desire which is itself more desirable than any other satisfaction." In his wisdom, Lewis added that joy "must be distinguished from happiness and pleasure."

Reader, can you imagine a God who dances with shouts of joy? The new Garden of Eden will be a place for a new kind of spiritual life that embraces joy. In the garden we will be awakened to God's presence. We will be relaxed and playful like children.

The joy of God is complete in every way. Nothing human or circumstantial adds to it or detracts from it. Joy is not made complete except through reliance and obedience to God. In Matthew Henry's commentary, joy is defined as "cheerfulness in conversation with our friends and a constant delight in God." John 3:29 says joy is the fulfillment of the promises and plans of God.

Louise Hay paints a word picture of what living with *jouissance* might mean. "In the infinity of life where I am, all is perfect, whole, and complete. Change is the natural law of my life. I welcome change. I am willing to change. I choose to change my thinking. I choose to change the words I use. I move from the old to the new with ease and joy. It is easier for me to forgive than I thought. Forgiving make me feel free and light. It is with joy that I learn to love myself more and more. The more resentment I release, the more love I have to express. Changing my thoughts makes me feel good. I am learning to make today a pleasure to experience. All is well in my world." (Louise Hay, *You Can Heal Your Life*, p. 95.)

We are able to experience joy in the times of trouble, trials, disease, persecution, and death. Read John 17. We can choose to experience *jousissance* and *chara*, even if we do not feel like it. Joy stays within us in good times and trying times. God wants each and every one to experience "the joy of the Lord" through walking in the garden with God until God comes to take us home.

Our culture teaches us to fight negative mentality. Fighting the negative absorbs our energy. The more we give attention to what we do not want, the more of it we create. What we place our attention on grows and becomes permanent.

That is what being saved is all about. That is what freedom in God really means. It is absolute freedom. Everything we do within God's divine purpose has been planned from the beginning. Walking with God in the cool of the garden in the new Eden will present to every soul what the precious beloved life can become. This highest joy is more than we will ever need or desire. There is more in living than the daily struggle filled with strife. Now we can freely breathe the air. God is the light at the end of the tunnel.

We are going home to Joy Land. I love the time when I can visit my East Tennessee family and friends. *Jouissance* is feeling home with our souls with who we are and what we have been doing. That feeling of familiar surroundings and the acceptance of friends is warm and comfortable. We are passing through in our life journey. This world is not our home. We are pilgrims going to an eternal city.

God has incredible plans for us. Embrace God with all your heart, mind, body, and soul.

Bibliography

Barash, Cathy, *Edible Flowers*. Golden, Colorado: Fulcrum Publishing, 1993.

Barr, James. *The Garden of Eden and the Hope of Immortality*. London: SCM, 1997.

Capon, Robert, *The Supper of the Lamb*. New York: Pocket Books, 1970.

Child, Julia. *People Who Love to Eat Are Always the Best People*. New York: Alfred A Knoph, 2020.

Claypool, John. *Tracks of a Fellow Struggler*. New York: Morehouse, 1974.

Deloria, Ella Cara. *Waterlily*. Lincoln: University of Nebraska Press, 1998.

Desjardins, Micheal. "Teaching About Religion with Food," *Teaching Theology and Religion* 7:3 (July 2004) 153-158.

Eliot, T.S. *Christianity and Culture*. New York: Jovanovich Books, 1960.

Gilmer, Maureen. *God in the Garden*. Chicago: Loyola Press, 2006.

Halwell, Brian. *Eat Here: Reclaiming the Pleasures of Locally Grown Food*. New York: Norton, 2004.

Harris, Maria. *Dance of the Spirit*. New York: Bantom Books, 1999.

Hay, Louise L. *You Can Heal Your Life*. Carlsbad, California: Hay House, 1999.

Kaplan, Justin. *Bartlett's Familiar Quotations*. Boston: Little, Brown Company, 1992.

Lemmel, Helen, "Turn Your Eyes Upon Jesus," 1922.

Lewis, C.S. *The Weight of Glory*. New York: Harper and Collins, 1980.

McFague, Sallie. *Life Abundant: Rethinking Theology and Economy for a Planet in Peril*. Minneapolis: Fortress Press, 2002.

McKenzie, Alec. *The Time Trap*. New York: American Management, 1997.

McTaggart, Lynne. *The Field: The Quest for the Secret Force of the Universe*. New York: Harper Collins, 2002.

Richardson, Alan. *The Theological Wordbook of the Bible*. New York: Mcmillian, 1960.

Shogren, Gary. "Is the Kingdom of God About Eating and Drinking (Romans14:17," *Novem Testamentum* 42:3(2000): 238-256.

Smith, Houston. "Reasons for Joy: The Soul of Christianity," *The Christian Century* 122:30 (October 4, 2005) 10-11.

Smith, Ken. *It's About Time: Getting Control of Your Life.* Chicago: Tyndale, 1998.

"The Way We Were" movie with words by Alan and Marilyn Bergman, 1973.

Thompson, Marjorie. *Soul Feast: An Invitation to the Christian Spiritual Life.* Louisville, Kentucky: Westminster Press, 2007.

Walker, Alice. *In Search of Our Mother's Garden.* Madison, Wisconsin: Turtleback Books, 1984.

Wigoder, Devorah. *The Garden of Eden Cookbook.* New York: Harper and Row, 2002.

Young, Robert. *Analytical Concordance to the Bible.* Peabody, Massachusetts: Henderson Publishers, 1999.

Zukav, Gary. *The Seat of the Soul.* New York: Fireside, 1990.

About the Author

"I'm just a human who is deeply in love with God. I enjoy walking with God in the garden. And the joy I share as I tarry there, no one will ever know." "Jimmy" enjoys writing, sports, eating, traveling, quiet times of prayer, and his family. He teaches and preaches God's Word with joy.

His first book, *Children in My Heart*, was published when he was 17. He has never stopped writing. In high school, he wrote and edited for the *Maroon and White*. In college he was religion editor for the *Orange and Blue*. He was the religion editor for the *Missourian* in Columbia. After journalism school and seminary, he wrote and used his gifts serving his denominational boards.

His books have been legion. His words have empowered the world with passionate practical messages. Dr. Norman Vincent Peale and Christ have anointed Jim as the minister of joy to the world.

www.ingramcontent.com/pod-product-compliance
Lightning Source LLC
Chambersburg PA
CBHW071502070526
44578CB00001B/416